Becoming

To Bennie —
with appreciation for your
beautiful soul
Love,

J.d

Becoming

An Introduction to Jung's Concept of Individuation

Deldon Anne McNeely

Becoming: An Introduction to Jung's Concept of Individuation

Published simultaneously in Canada and the United States of America. For
information on obtaining permission for use of material from this work,
submit a written request to: permissions@fisherkingpress.com

Fisher King Press
PO Box 222321
Carmel, CA 93922
www.fisherkingpress.com
info@fisherkingpress.com
+1-831-238-7799

Preface

Becoming reflects my hope to leave my grandchildren and others of their generation an understanding of the ideas of Carl Gustav Jung. His idea of a process called individuation has sustained my dedication to my lifelong work of psychoanalysis, and it saddens me that the principles that guided me have been dismissed by the current trends in psychology and psychiatry.

We psychotherapists know the value of Jung's approach through clinical results, that is, watching people enlarge their consciousness and change their attitudes and behavior, transforming their suffering into psychological well-being.

Psychology's fascination with behavioral techniques, made necessary by financial concerns and promoted by insurance companies and pharmaceutical companies, has changed the nature of psychotherapy and has attempted to dismiss the wisdom of Jung and other pioneers of the territory of the unconscious mind. We psychoanalysts have played a part in the loss by not transmitting our message clearly. For a combination of unfortunate circumstances, many of the younger generation, including college and medical students, are deprived of fully understanding their own minds. Those with a scientific bent are sometimes turned away from self-reflection by the suggestion that unconscious processes are metaphysical mumbo-jumbo. Superficial assessments of Jung have led to the incorrect conclusion that one must be a spiritual seeker, or religious, in order to follow Jung's ideas about personality. I would like to correct that impression.

Some university professors tell me that they are not allowed to teach Jungian psychology. Secular humanism and positivism have shaped the academic worldview; therefore, investigation into the unknown or unfamiliar dimensions of human experience is not valued. But this attitude contrasts with the positive reputation Jung enjoys among therapists, artists of all types, and philosophers. Those without resistance to the unconscious because of their creativity, open-mindedness, or personal disposition are more likely to receive Jung's explorations without prejudice or ideological resistance. There is a lively conversation going on about Jung's ideas in journals and conferences among diverse groups of thinkers which does not reach mainstream psychology.

Becoming is for those whose minds are receptive to the unknown, and I hope it will help some of us to think—more with respect than dread—of the possibility that we act unconsciously.

In organizing this book, I wanted to prepare for understanding "individuation" by identifying the historical and philosophical contexts in which Jung was situated, and then addressing the question of where this approach fits with the cultural issues of today. If we were reading this as a play, Part I would set the stage and introduce the main characters. Part II describes the action of individuation as it presents itself on the current cultural stage. Part III is like director's notes for those who have curiosity for more discussion; it amplifies the basic ideas in each chapter and is called "Lagniappe." This term, common in Louisiana, means you will get a little something extra, like a thirteenth donut when buying a dozen. It is not necessary to read Part III in order to understand why I find the concept of individuation important for each of us, but it is a little something extra that some may enjoy.

Acknowledgements

Karen Farley has made this book possible, and my gratitude for her help knows no bounds. Her writing skills provided valuable editing, her computer skills enabled me to get the manuscript to the publisher, her intelligent appreciation of Jung supported me throughout the process of shaping my ideas for print, and her generosity and patience are extraordinary. Curtis Brooks has also been invaluable in his careful editing and generosity in discussing ideas.

I am very grateful to those who read the manuscript in its early stages and gave important criticism and encouragement, Clare and Peter Kearney, William Doty, Everett McLaren, and Nancy Cater. You enabled me to trust the work.

I thank those who were so valuable in working with me on parts of the manuscript, Sue Crommelin, Jerome Bernstein, Chandler Dennis, Mary Barron, Ron Kledzik, David Sedgwick, and Tim Sanderson.

To Mel Mathews of Fisher King Press, my sincere gratitude for being available and collaborative.

Contents

Part 1

Introduction

Becoming

I

A Question of Principle

I inquire, I do not assert; I do not here determine anything with final assurance; I conjecture, try, compare, attempt, ask...

(This comment by an alchemist, quoted by C.G. Jung in volume 16 of his *Collected Works*, captures the spirit of Jung's work and also of this project.)

Is there a principle of order operating throughout the universe, or are we all embedded in chaos? A pioneer in psychoanalysis, psychiatrist C.G. Jung, did not claim to have proof that there was such a principle, but he observed that, no matter what they believe, humans *behave* as if such a principle exists, and have done so throughout history and throughout all cultures.

Jung found that the *idea* of an ordering principle occurred in all cultures and that human behavior reflected an assumption of such a principle. He called that idea the "Self." He noted that as the body operates as a unit organizing a number of systems, so the psychic functions are organized by a unifying force. He proposed that our psychological life's work—becoming an integrated person, our "individuation"—is to learn how that principle of order manifests in us, to become more familiar with this Self that seems to influence our behavior. This principle or force has been known as the inner voice, a higher power, the dream-maker, the greater self, the mysterious "other" in our personality, the divine spark, the beloved, or destiny; but whatever it is called, many people recognize that something within them beyond their ordinary plans for themselves influences their lives.

Throughout this paper I will capitalize "Self" to distinguish it from the commonplace meaning of "self" that denotes a particular personality organization, as in "myself." "Self" with capital "S" is not an idea about something that is just personal. "Self" as Jung uses it has compli-

cated implications. We can think of it as the principle that gives organization and unity to our personality. But then, if we wonder, "Where
does such a principle originate?" our perception widens. We can choose
to believe it originates in human nature purely on a biological level,
like a thermostat; or we can see it as implying a connection to some
force beyond the human, a transpersonal random cosmic force; or we
can imagine yet a connection to a superhuman intelligent source or
divinity.

The Self, however we imagine it, might extend beyond a personal
consciousness to include all of human consciousness and all that lies
beyond us. But does Jung's "Self" make sense any longer? Not everyone
is comfortable thinking in such grand terms as "universal principles."
Self could be simply a chance consequence of evolution causing humans to create sensible stories that tie experiences together meaning-
fully, even though there is no reasonable order "out there." Rather than
having a blueprint for our development as a person, the Self might
merely keep adapting to whatever we choose to be at the moment.

A lot happened in the century after Jung made the idea of individuation his motif. Up and down, in and out, good and bad, male and
female—designations like those would not stay in place, raising suspi-
cions about an ordering principle. Sounds of the Big Bang were detected
by scientists but denied by anti-scientists who question the reality of
research. The moon was brought down to earth. We discovered how
to make life in a lab and also how to wipe the world away utterly and
in a flash. Kingdoms, forests, and languages were deconstructed. Cam-
eras were swallowed, showing us enemies we hid inside ourselves. Brain
scans revealed infants' intrauterine conversations with their mothers.
Women wore their underwear on the outside, and men took off their
armor and tucked it inside. Physicists trying to form consistent theories
about the universe became more and more confused and entangled.
The philosopher says we killed God, but the priest says he hears Something laughing. It is hard to tell our children what's what!

Jung thought that human nature was shaped by the Self acting
within each personality and that our individuation occurred when we
became conscious of cooperating with the Self. Being in touch with
the Self would keep a person feeling whole, as opposed to feeling frag-
mented; it would be a source of stability as well as creative energy in
the face of outer disorganization. My purpose here is to clarify the idea

of individuation; even if we have no background in psychology or philosophy, each of us can decide if it survives the chaos of contemporary thought. May the spirit of W.B. Yeats help us! The poet wrote:

> Hands, do what you're bid:
> Bring the balloon of the mind
> That bellies and drags in the wind
> Into its narrow shed.

So let us bring our balloon minds to the task, trying to tie to earth airy words and ideas.

Jung was deliberately vague in his description of the nature of the process so as to avoid too literal interpretations. He did not want to encourage "recipes" or oversimplified directions for what had to be a particularly unique process for each one of us.

In simplest form, individuation means choosing to be conscious, or mindful, and especially, it means becoming conscious of the person we are capable of being in our fullness, our strengths, and our limitations.

Is the concept of a process of individuation relevant in the 21st century? Some look into the chaos and say, "No, it is not; a principle of order seems to be missing from too many lives." Others say, "Yes, even in times of chaos, life continues to try to heal into harmony."

> Probably as in all metaphysical questions, both are true:
> Life is—or has—meaning and meaninglessness. I cherish
> the anxious hope that meaning will preponderate and win
> the battle. (Jung, *Memories, Dreams, Reflections*, p. 359.)

Perhaps after reading this you will be better able to decide that for yourself. If it is relevant, what is individuation now and what does the Self want for or from you?

2

Avoiding Recipes, Accepting Responsibility

In his autobiography, Jung describes his first reaction to reading al-chemical texts: "Good Lord, what nonsense! This stuff is impossible to understand!" (Jung, *Memories, Dreams, Reflections*, p. 204.)

I had a similar reaction to my first Jungian lecture, and I see in the way listeners' eyes glaze over at some Jungian presentations that it's not unusual to respond to Jungian thought this way in the beginning. A frequent criticism of Jung's writing is that he delves into obscure stuff, such as alchemy, that is not current and practical. What's important to keep in mind is that later Jung realized the alchemists were thinking in symbols and describing the individuation process as they imagined it; he saw the momentous value of what was being conveyed and found it exciting. As Jung stuck with studying alchemy, I stuck with studying Jung in spite of that first reaction. I hope you will stick with this too, as I will try to present the idea of individuation so as to minimize confu-sion.

It is crucial that we do not confuse *individuation* and *individualism*. The "know thyself" of Socrates does not translate to "It's all about *Me!*" Individuation implies something other than maturation, good self-es-teem, good adjustment, success, or fame. It involves restructuring the mind.

As individuals, these are times of mixed messages about what is of value, messages that come from such a variety of influences—from the markets of pop culture, health gurus, spiritual growth advisors, and re-ligious institutions, even from the army: Be all that you can be! Every few months a new book catches hold of the public imagination, and millions of us throng to acquire it and the knowledge that will give us the "purposeful life," the "secret" of life, the ten things that will make us make something of ourselves. How do we determine which paths to follow in becoming the person we are meant to be? Where should we put our energies and effort? Are there goals that will stand up to the vagaries of changing times and the aging process? Should we aim for balance or passion, for stability or adaptability? Should I spend time and money analyzing myself or just take a pill and buy a new car?

There are similarities in many of these messages, and I will be trying to explain why I chose Jung's method to follow for myself. It is not the only way. Try to keep an open mind and remember that wise people have been thinking and speaking about these things forever. Of course, as my philosopher friend Bill Brenner says, "If your mind is too open, nothing can stay in it," so you are entitled to an opinion!

Step one: Become aware of the possibility of a relationship to the Self—as if the Self were an intelligible entity—and learn to speak with it. How? Theoretically the Self has access to our unconscious thoughts and feelings, while our egos know only our conscious thoughts and feelings. Through unexpected meetings with the unconscious processes, this unknown part of nature can be identified and engaged. This does not mean that we listen to some inner voice and obey anything it asks. I am speaking about having a conversation, even at times a debate with the Self.

There is a very practical reason for listening to our unconscious in the form of dreams and intuitions. As they connect us to unknown parts of ourselves, they can be life-savers. A friend dreamed that she was attacked in the chest with a foreign object. Since she was experiencing some mild changes in pulse rate, the dream spurred her on to have herself checked. Tests showed that she had a serious growth on her heart. Her condition was corrected by surgery, but, had it been ignored, probably would have killed her. Often a dream will warn you about a physical condition before your waking mind is aware of it.

Intuition sometimes warns us of dangers—dangerous decisions, people, and situations—that we would otherwise overlook. We can probably remember times when we had a warning feeling about someone who did prove to be untrustworthy or dangerous. We can't be sure of such intuitions—they can be wrong—but we should pay attention and check them out.

A patient was thrilled and yet uncomfortable (his intuition) about the pious woman he was in love with. She seemed to be in love with him too, so he couldn't understand why he was anxious. Then a dream supported his intuition: he dreamed that she was driving them recklessly. The car was heading for a cliff when he woke in a panic. Sobered from his state of infatuated elation, he began to ask more questions and be more realistic about her values. He found that despite her reputation as a religious person, she was quite impulsive, had been dishonest about her accomplishments and, in fact, had a history of treating people destructively.

Besides dreams and intuitions, we become aware of the Self and the unconscious by paying attention to our strong passions and attractions, but also our uncomfortable feelings and reactions, like fear, jealousy, irritations, hatreds, envy, and physical symptoms—not just noticing them, but questioning their source. Why does this person's manner evoke a rage in me that has no reasonable explanation? What aspect of me does that person represent? Why do I always get a headache on Saturday morning? To seriously examine the question is to look at *why* we feel as we do, and not to automatically dismiss an experience as chance or say, "Because it's *true*." "Because he *is* annoying!" "It's a coincidence." "That's just the way I am."

Being in touch with the Self can affect your mental and physical health and can prevent your hiding from yourself and placing blame on others.

But beyond our own personal well-being, is the concept of individuation important for the human species? Jung feared that we as a human race were heading toward an impending catastrophe. He thought that by evolving psychologically we might be able to avoid and/or survive the threatening apocalypse, the collapse of civilized life. Jung is not alone is his concern about human survival. In an online essay about the development of intelligent life in the universe, the physicist Stephen Hawking said, "I shall take this to include the human race, even though much of its behaviour through out history has been pretty stupid, and not calculated to aid the survival of the species." (Hawking, "Life in the Universe," January, 2009.) Raising human consciousness is the key to making life on earth survivable, thought Jung.

The survival of the race as we know it is of questionable value. We are potentially capable of destroying our own planet and others. We are potentially capable of programming ourselves into cyborgs. Some consider the expanding human population to be a blight or virus on the earth, a failed experiment. Let us not debate this here, but assume that many of us wish that humans will survive, if not improve in our humanity.

Some argue that Jung is the most important psychologist of our century in that he pointed us to the *creative powers* that lie in the universal pool of knowledge in which we all participate. These creative powers are what we will either call on to rescue us from utter destruction of the race, or abandon along with humanity itself, or at least acknowledge as our companions in facing the unknown. Jung used the phrase "collective psyche." It means essentially "the information present in the human race as a whole"—that information stored in our DNA, our memories, our brains, our cells, our instincts, and our common images and languages. "Collective unconscious," "objective psyche," and "collective psyche" are Jung's terms that all mean the same thing, the sum total of the human race's psychological experience.

The ability to learn from history is something we have often been too absorbed with ourselves to do. The connection with previous ages, with previous civilizations and empires, with our ancestors, with nature, and with future possibilities, all available to us in the collective psyche if we could only listen, would help our survival. This is a subject dear to many thoughtful scholars, a recent example being Jared Diamond. In his book, *Collapse: How Societies Choose to Fail or Succeed,* Diamond illustrates the effect of unconsciousness on the fate of many specific extinct civilizations. With attention to civilizations before us, we could be more enlightened about cultures and peoples of the world today, and about how our values interact.

More than that, Jung gave us a reason to believe that each of us is a participant in the cosmic creation responsible for adding to the consciousness of the universe. Perhaps each of us, by coming to know our own relationship to Self, contributes to the pool of consciousness in the universe. Each of us capable of understanding this has a responsibility for the evolution of mindfulness.

For example, when I think "an eye for an eye, a tooth for a tooth," I think only about my personal pride. It is a leap of consciousness to realize that pure vengeance is a dead end. There were conditions when an attitude of dog-eat-dog, survival-at-any-cost, made sense. Information and resources were limited and strangers were a threat. But the world has shrunk and the human family is closely contained and connected; a different attitude is called for. Refusal to take revenge means thinking beyond mere pride in physical survival and seeing a larger picture that includes respecting the rights of others. If I take that leap, I begin to see something more useful in negotiating than in destroying my enemy. It is possible that that bit of increased consciousness contributes to the consciousness of the whole, as each drop of water contributes to the sea.

Being curious—about your neighbor's welfare, your nation's policies toward the rest of the world, the welfare of other animal species and ecological systems, the condition of the planet—raises the level of consciousness of the whole by a little bit. This theme is explored in many art forms; see for example, the recent movies "Freedom Writers" and "Crash." In both movies the subjects of the stories were provoked to see beyond their personal needs into a larger worldview and an expansion of their capacity for compassion.

Early Greece produced plays that reflected such growth in awareness. Dionysus, the god of the renewal, symbolized by the grapevine, presided over many aspects of nature, including intoxication and madness. In early times he was celebrated with wild, drunken orgies, but as Greek civilization advanced and turned violence into art, the celebrations of Dionysus evolved into festivals of theatre. In their dramas the playwrights showed how generations of one family could be dominated by envy, vengeance, and murder, until an evolution of consciousness resulted in a system of justice. The patricides, fratricides, sacrificing of children, and slaying of enemies was replaced by a sense of restraint that allowed cooler heads to judge what was deemed fair. The Greeks gave credit to the gods for teaching them the advanced attitudes. Now we would say humans advance in consciousness through the awareness of potential benefits to all, through being Self-centric instead of egocentric.

These concerns, these everyday problems that we might bring to therapy, or the larger issues of the welfare of our species, are understandable. But what of timeless, transpersonal goals, the ultimate purposes of existence? Some psychologists feel this is a valid subject of psychology. Others do not. They criticize Jung for discussing psychology in relation to anthropology, religion, physics, astrology, sociology, literature, and so on. Most psychologists and therapists accept the physical and psychological dimensions of his ideas, but many do not accept the transcendent dimension, or at least do not think it a proper subject for psychology.

When we consider a transcendent dimension, we enlarge the psychological to include a sacred dimension. Some believe that Jung showed us that the ultimate goal of human psychological development is to find our place within a cosmic unity. He thought the physical and psychological, matter and mind, humans and nature, make up one, holistic reality. Within that cosmic unity is our image of a god. Perhaps God is not dead, but our image of God is changing. In that case, instead of blindly accepting an image of the divine from outside sources, such as a religious dogma, we would be actually responsible for changing our image of God by meeting and having dialogue with the Self.

For Jung, by becoming aware of a relationship with the Self, each individual is not abandoned to suffer the existential emptiness of individualism, but ultimately finds in his individual soul the presence of a whole universe and a relationship to its timelessness. We could come to discover and transform aspects of a spiritual presence in us through our own efforts to communicate with the Self. Some psychologists believe that the transcendent dimension could help us survive by creating a more tolerant and less selfish society. We could step outside of our personal values and see into the holiness of all of creation. We could feel connected to and responsible for all of creation.

But positing a transcendent dimension raises another issue. A conscious, unified universe can result from an intelligence that resides in man alone, or it can be the result of an intelligence that comes from a source beyond human consciousness. Analytical Psychology, as Jung's model of psychology is called, allows both a secular and a sacred character. Both presuppose a dimension of reality that is conscious, but one presumes that that consciousness is purposeful and intelligent.

The feeling that the Self is "other" opens the possibility that the "other" is a product of human consciousness alone, a secular theory; or the "other" may be a consciousness beyond the human, a divine intelligence, a spiritual theory. Secular and spiritual theories are more than just names. They result in different human behavior. A secular society seeks information and understanding and reduces anxiety through knowing. A spiritual society seeks mystery and reduces anxiety by not needing to know.

Secular humanism values human life and dignity and finds in those values enough reason to live a decent and even altruistic life without calling on the idea of divinity to support it. It does not require a relationship with the spiritual dimension to justify its values and does not support religious expressions of spirituality.

One of the assets of Jung's theory is that no one is obliged to accept the transcendent or spiritual dimension, but neither are we prohibited from including it as some ideologies would demand. For example, Freud considered the need for a spiritual life a weakness, wishful thinking, a defense against anxiety. Marxism denigrates religion, "the opiate of the masses," believing that it weakens rather than strengthens the validity of the community. According to Marx, religions reflect an unhealthy superstition which undermines pragmatic social action. In contrast to these theories, Jung believed that any psychological experience was worth studying seriously. He posited a religious instinct as part of the natural psyche and believed that many of the ills of today were the result of our having lost touch with our deep spiritual resources. We don't know if Jung believed that the Self extends beyond the human dimension. He may have been agnostic, or an atheist. What he believed is not relevant; he urged each of us to find our inner truth. In Analytical Psychology we are invited to explore the spiritual dimension.

In the secular understanding, the Self is a hypothetical construct, a working concept that can be explained on a biological level. It can be seen simply as a description of the way the human mind works without implying anything about the existence of things spiritual. There is much to be learned from Jung on a level of psychological theory, so that if you are a humanist or atheist you can find meaning there. The universe may be a vast being, evolving without a plan but steered by human intelligence.

The Self can also imply the existence of a dimension of reality that is intelligent and purposeful and that is not produced by human physical and cultural movements—in fact, is independent of human nature and, therefore, sacred. Those who imagine the Self this way experience it as divine and might give it images and names of gods, goddesses, or other divine figures. They can picture themselves in constant intimate union with this divinity or separate, emotionally detached, and respectful of it.

In either case, there is no point outside of the psyche from which to view the psyche, so there is no scientific answer to the question of whether a transcendent dimension exists. Even if we imagine a divine being responsible for the universe, humanists would point out that that does not provide any answers as to the origin of the divine. Either approach ends in mystery. Jung imagined that there could be some way of answering the question at some distant time in our evolution and that physics might advance to find such an answer.

This discussion of Jung's contribution to the survival of the species is not meant to imply that Jung's is the only message that can support our survival or that he alone is a messiah of psychological awareness. We will consider how his way of describing development is consistent with some other paths to fulfillment, and how it differs from some as well.

• • •

The life of Buddha is an example of individuation. He was privileged and enjoyed every possible means of comfort and pleasure, sheltered from want. What moved him to want to experience the world beyond his palace? He went into the world of ordinary people and found sickness, poverty, and suffering. It seemed he felt his life was not complete until he had experienced the dark and sordid side of life. Only then could he fulfill his destiny as a spiritual sage. His life illustrates the idea that we are not completed by being good or by having what seems like perfection. Individuation as completion means filling out all of our possible conscious experiences and being aware of our potential, the pleasant and unpleasant, good and bad.

3

Reality of the Psyche

In 1965, Jolande Jacobi, Jung's colleague, wrote *The Way of Individuation*, now a classic. We can use it as a source for delving into questions that speak to us a half-century later. During that half-century the blooming of modernism, post-modernism, and post-post-modern thought raised questions and nuances that color and complicate our images of individuation as presented by Jacobi.

Jung saw himself as a scientific observer of human behavior, not a philosopher who speculated about truth. Still, he was influenced by his own philosophical orientation, as we all are whether we know it or not. We are products of the dominant philosophies of our century, our society, our family, our education. Before adopting anyone's opinions as our own, we should consider what influenced them. Jung wrote:

> Although I owe not a little to philosophy, and have ben-
> efited by the rigorous discipline of its methods of thought,
> I nevertheless feel in its presence that holy dread which is
> inborn in every observer of facts. ("Foreword to Mehlich,
> 'Fichte's Psychology and Its Relation to the Present,'" CW
> 18, par. 1730.)

Many of us approach philosophy with holy dread. Its depth threatens to drown us in a confusion of ideas. Jung tried to limit himself to observable facts rather than philosophical speculations. He discussed the concept of individuation in many places throughout his writings, but always guarded against being specific about a process that was meant to serve the particular truth of each individual. So his descriptions of the Self as both the initiator of growth and the endpoint, or we can say, the motivator as well as the goal of individuation, also were vague enough to leave much to speculation.

In order to grasp Jung's intentions, we have to accept his image of himself as an empiricist—one who deals with observable facts, rather than a metaphysician—one who deals with unseen, non-physical subjects. He insisted that he was not talking about supernatural phenomena, the nature of God, or religion. Nor did he claim to be a theologian. If he spoke of God, it was the image of God found in the minds of his subjects of observation. He spoke of the "reality of the psyche." What does that mean?

From the beginning of time humans have described their images of the literal or observable world and also of imaginal or spiritual worlds. Though a spiritual world can never be proven by reason, the human psyche persists in imaging and conceiving of a world beyond its concrete experience. Many think of that world as infinite, despite the fact that we have no way of conceiving of infinity through experience. We can only understand infinity by its absence from our experience, through our imagination. This consistent experience of trusting something beyond the senses, of transcending mere physical experience in our imagination, despite the absence of "actual" confirmation, is what Jung called the "reality of the psyche."

If you have a "mathematical mind," you are attracted to certain abstract notions, like the notion of infinity, or principles of ordering of numbers by formula. Mathematics is founded on a belief in the regularity of truth. As mathematics becomes advanced, it works in a world of symbols whose meanings are obscure to non-mathematicians, but are real enough to be discovered, repeated, and related in some deep way to the working of the material world. This is the "reality of numbers."

For a physicist, reality is more than meets the senses. We live in a world of such complexity, only available to us through the imagination. The typical illustration of this complexity of ordinary objects from the standpoint of subatomic particles in constant motion is often presented as considering a physical object as resembling "a bowl of jello." (Bartusiak, *Einstein's Unfinished Symphony*, p. 146.)

Similarly, if you have a "psychological mind," you are attracted to abstract notions of the landscape of the psyche/soul. "Psychology" from the Greek, means "the study of soul." Yet these days, some scientists may not tolerate the use of the word "soul" as the subject of psychology, and the more acceptable word is "mind." But we cannot refer to "mind" in the same way psychologists did years ago when the "mind" was considered fairly well differentiated from the body. Neither can we limit "mind" to brain substance. Now we think of "mind" as a complex function that includes networks of information from inside (nerve messages, chemicals carried in the bloodstream, et cetera) and outside of the body (visual and auditory sources of information, stimuli, conditioning, et cetera).

To further complicate the study of mind, the subject, the mind, is also the student! This creates weird loops, paradoxes, and resonances within the being of the psychologist that can be dizzying! Looking at ourselves, we look into a hall of mirrors.

We are tantalized by trying to find the "I" that does the looking. We call that "I" the ego, but we come to see that the ego is not the only "eye" in the psyche. Depth psychology sees that the ego revolves around a point that is both in it and around it. The ego revolves around the Self as the earth revolves around the sun. How can that be understood?

We can observe ourselves and our mirror-minds and souls through many lenses. From the lens of particle physics we explore the elements of consciousness at the microscopic level, dissecting and stimulating the brain. This is a valuable and necessary investigation in understanding our world, but it has no practical application for a parent, a baseball player, or a therapist at this stage of knowledge. There is no way we can apply what we learn about brain cells from the microscope, no matter how interesting, to living life in the moment.

We can explore consciousness through a larger lens which studies how the brain and bodily systems produce our abstract concepts, such as a consistent sense of self. This research we can apply on an individual basis to help us understand our behavior, but it is generally out of our hands as far as helping us make decisions or accepting responsibility. For example, we may see how the brain's amygdala communicates with its prefrontal cortex, and how that affects our decision-making processes. That may be helpful in understanding the effect of a brain injury or drug incident, but that is not especially useful in an urgent instant of decision making.

A wider lens looks at the interactions of that self with society and its place in the human system. Here we begin to assert an aspect of freedom of choice. As creatures that have an impact on other creatures, we make decisions that can be examined and judged. We may have limited choices of behavior—not total free will, but we have some choice.

An even wider lens, the lens of depth psychology, attempts to abstract farther into human consciousness as it affects and is affected by movement in the universe that reaches beyond our present day human society, into history, culture, and religion.

In the words of Jung:

> All our knowledge consists of stuff of the psyche—which, because it alone is immediate, is superlatively real. Here, then, is a reality to which the psychologist can appeal— namely psychic reality...Psychic contents are derived from the "material" environment; as when I picture the car I want to buy. Others, no less real, seem to come from a "spiritual" source which appears to be very different from the physical environment, such as wondering about the state of the soul of my dead father. My fear of a ghost is a psychic image just as real to me as my fear of fire. We don't try to account for our fear of either one by physical arguments, but we experience each of them as real... Unless we accept the reality of the psyche we try to explain our experiences in a way that does violence to many of them— those (experiences) expressed through superstition, religion, and philosophy. Truth that appeals to the testimony of the senses may satisfy reason, but it offers nothing that stirs our feelings and expresses them by giving a meaning to human life. ("Basic Postulates of Analytical Psychology," CW 8, par. 680-686.)

We human beings have been portraying ourselves repeatedly in literature and myth as part animal, part angel; or as occupying the space between heaven and earth. From ancient to contemporary times, human thought has gravitated between what appears to be a duality: physical reality (phenomena, representations, matter) and an otherworldly reality of "forms" (noumena, ideals, essences, universals). The earliest philosophers, like Plato, could speak authoritatively of the soul, of immortality, infinity, of a world of "forms" or ideals. From them we learned to speak about "eternal truths"—the value of honesty, loyalty, bravery, justice—that they are in the mind; they cannot be demonstrated to result from logical facts. They are abstractions, but they are real values.

A famous lesson in the abstract value of honesty is Plato's story of the Ring of Gyges, a ring that renders one invisible and leads its owner to utter selfishness. Gyges, a poor shepherd, unexpectedly comes upon the ring on a corpse and steals it. Realizing that it makes him invisible, he uses its power to take whatever he wants. He steals the king's gold and even his wife, and becomes king. Plato uses this to illustrate "egoism," a form of moral skepticism. Yet we recognize that another attitude is possible, an attitude that considers that Gyges could have chosen not to use his powers dishonestly. Perhaps he would not have achieved much, but he might have chosen to be honest. The story prompts us to reflect on the human tendency to pursue selfish goals rather than look at a more abstract value. An extreme of skepticism would be to say dismissively, "Honesty is just an abstract concept in the mind. It does not otherwise exist."

If no one could see you, would you do good? Why, or why not?

Immanuel Kant concluded his *Critique of Practical Reason* (1788) with these memorable words: "Two things fill the mind with ever new and increasing admiration and awe, the more often and steadily we reflect upon them: the starry heavens above me and the moral law within me."

In the next chapter we will do a whirlwind tour, skimming through centuries of the history of philosophy as it broadly relates to psychology. Fasten your seatbelts if you choose to look into this historical context of Analytical Psychology.

4

A Philosophical Moment

I'm no longer quite sure what the question is, but I do know that the answer is "Yes."

–Leonard Bernstein

Western philosophy begins in ancient Greece. It does not include centuries of Asian thought. Psychology today values the contribution of Asian philosophy; we will look more at this in later chapters.

In the last chapter, we considered the early age of philosophy and the concern for finding a relationship between matter and spirit. The solution for Plato was a dual world, one physical and one spiritual. Plato thought of soul as existing in its own world of forms, but when Stoics, Epicureans, and Skeptics spoke of soul, they considered it one with the life-force of the body. Some denied the notion that the soul could live on after death. Their pragmatic views were dominant in Roman society.

A basic question is: Are matter and energy united, or is there a separation between the spirit world and physical world? Many religions prefer a view of spiritual beings and God as existing in a realm apart from the physical. Others, including Jung, say that, although we don't yet understand how, spirit and matter are united aspects of one world.

Today the no-nonsense tenets of modern skeptics deny the existence of the spiritual and find expression in short-term pragmatic solutions to problems, including behavioral therapies. Skeptics are not likely to embrace psychodynamic or any other long-term therapy, but are available when discipline and action are called for. Some prisoners of war found courage and consolation, even through years of solitary confinement, by recalling the life of the Stoic, Epictetus, whose writings justified to the common Roman soldier why we suffer for the sake of our convictions.

Long-term psychodynamic psychotherapy respects the need for quick solutions to particular, discrete problems but also acknowledges the importance of the whole history of relationships in a person's life, as well as the seriousness of one's spiritual beliefs.

Belief in an immortal soul was popular in ancient Greece but doubted in the more materialistic Roman thought. As Christianity became popular, the bias swung back toward believing in an immortal soul inhabiting its material vessel, the body. This belief prevailed throughout the Middle Ages while the human being was the center of the world and was identified with his relationship to the keeper of his soul, the Church. Morality plays, such as "Everyman," are still performed and still have the emotional force of those times as we see a person struggling to realize his own soul's worth.

But a revolution in knowledge occurred: the astronomers Copernicus and Galileo proved that the sun, not the earth, was the center of the universe. Gradually the Christian church, which had tried to squelch this knowledge (by imprisoning Galileo, for example), was forced to relinquish its power as holder of truth. Now belief was in the hands of intellectual reasoning and scientific data. The coming of this era, the Enlightenment, stressed the contrasting value of physical reality over psychic reality, of the authority of reason over the authority of the clergy, and of the scientific method of induction from facts to generalizations (instead of deduction from intuitive generalizations to facts). A culture of rationalism took hold.

Now this cultural era also had its opposition. In response to the emphasis on reason, machines, and sense data, the movement called Romanticism and the return to nature became strongly influential. Here Freud (to some extent) and Jung took their stand. They insisted that man is not just a machine but is a dynamic and complicated being that is influenced by psychological forces unknown to us through reason alone. So we see these opposing trends—one emphasizing physical reality and the other psychic reality—continuing to alternate in predominance throughout history.

The American psychologist William James noted the tendency of philosophers to fall into either of two camps, the "tough-minded" pragmatists or the "tender-minded" idealists. Jung, too, wrestled with the fact that different personality types think and feel differently about philosophical issues. Each type has certain biases. Jung worked out a more complicated system of personality types than James had, but they are similar. The fundamental types in Jung's system are introversion and extraversion.

Though there are many outlets for idealists and intuitive minds who are attracted to psychic reality in our society, tough-minded materialism prevails in many official institutions, including the medical establishment. The predominance of pharmacological treatment in psychiatry today underlines the bias toward materialistic views of the personality. Yet the attraction to psychic reality persists in spite of the bias toward physical medicine, and a huge counterculture to allopathic medicine exists in followers of alternative medicine.

Another way of describing the dichotomy in human experience began with the ancient Greeks, who contrasted the gods Dionysus and Apollo. Dionysus represents instinctual spontaneity and Apollo represents reasonable restraint and order. In Dionysus we join with nature and disregard individuality, while in Apollo we protect ourselves from being swallowed up by nature. And another view of the same idea is the image of centrifugal and centripetal energies at the heart of existence; there is continual tension between a unifying, centripetal, integrative force, and a decentralizing, differentiating, and pluralistic centrifugal force.

The period of the nineteenth and twentieth centuries, when the cultures of Western nations were dominated by Enlightenment ideals—preference for reason and science—is called "modernity." The prominence of rational science and the consequent disillusionment with religion was followed by a tendency toward spiritual nihilism. This movement came to prominence during Jung's lifetime in the early 20th century, the age of modernity. In the mid-twentieth century some philosophers and artists reacted to the overly confident rationalism of modernity by questioning and deconstructing all that seemed "certain" and showing us how false or phony our concepts and our belief in absolutes could be. This was considered the beginning of the post-modern movement and deconstruction. Minimalism ruled and satire and irony flourished, bringing the words "punk" and "grunge" into popularity and throwing a veil over an abyss of genuine sadness and frustrated love.

The veil of satire and irony is welcome relief from Victorian saccharine sentimentality and also from the pressure of too much structure and too much disappointment in failing structures. But eventually irony and satire grow tiresome, and then begins the longing for sincerity and genuine emotions.

Now in the 21st century a new wave has come along. Deconstruction and the absence of hope and possibility that accompanies nihilism have given way to a fascination with mystery. While mystery is still avoided in academia, the public seems to seek it, as we see by the popularity of movies and books about "Harry Potter," "The Da Vinci Code," "Lord of the Rings," "Tales of Narnia," "The Matrix," and the whole genre of science-fiction with its other dimensions of idealists and evil doers.

As I write this in 2008-2009, we are in a very interesting period in psychology, philosophy, physics, and the arts. It is as if deconstruction wiped away a lot of excessive and flowery nonsense and left us, not with empty garbage as some feared, but with a greater respect for our ignorance. The minds of many people are not content to accept answers about reality from the "experts," and, the more we question, the more in awe we become of the fragility of humanity's place in the cosmos. To this we have a choice to respond with dread or gratitude.

One of the interesting things that both William James and Jung discovered in investigating personality types is that each type experiences the other's type as inferior. This seems to be the case for worldviews, where another's world appears as a kind of trap. Spiritual seekers perceive materialism as an empty prison. Materialists find nothing but sick delusion in a religious attitude. We can see that these differences in temperament, attitudes, and thinking styles have operated in human society since earliest history. By creating conflicts and opposition, they spur us on to new dialogue. Progress in knowledge does not come only through cooperation, but also from competition and contention.

Although this theoretical division reveals an oppositional mindset that appears inevitable given its long-standing presence and emotional intensity, respect for differences and mutual understanding are possible if we are willing to open a dialogue and share information. An example of cooperative research is the neurological study of human development, which indicates that the psychological has a direct effect on the physical.

For example, the attitude and behavior of parents during the first years of life substantially influences the size and rate of their child's brain growth. Later influences and attitudes also affect bodily structures.

On the social level a change in information and the psychological priorities of a society can dramatically change the physical behavior and lifestyles of its members. In twenty years we have seen big changes in ecology as a result of information about global warming. Stewarding of energy resources is changing the way many people decide to spend their time and money, vote on taxes, choose the cars they buy and the trips they take. The development of contraceptives changed sexual behavior globally. Information about sexually transmitted diseases persuaded many to change their behavior. It seems that if we continue to gather information about how humans grow and function, and if we are also sensitive enough to think reflectively about issues, we might bridge the divide between the apparent polarities of physical and psychological reality.

Actually, as long as we acknowledge the fallibility of human reason, several different worldviews are possible for depth psychologists. We can imagine the fact of human consciousness as a chance development in the evolution of purposeless forces and still appreciate and be curious about that development. Or we can agree with sages who say that the fact that human consciousness exists is convincing evidence that a higher consciousness exists in which we participate. Or we can take an agnostic stand and see life as a collection of humanly devised language games that render the question of meaning to be meaningless.

What forces drive your consciousness? Do you relate to the forces that move you as to blind, indifferent matter? Do you see them as mere inventions of your human mind? Or is there a supernatural quixotic demon playing with us in a cosmic laboratory? a benevolent spirit? an unfathomable mystery? No matter what you believe, you can find a purely factual and humanistic psychological theory to help you study human consciousness. However, the differences between worldviews appear when we leave the realm of natural psychological functioning and begin to conceive of ultimate goals, the transcendent possibilities. To assume a transcendent level of belief requires a leap to a different level of psychic processing that is not for everyone.

Poets can reach beyond philosophy, and, as here, point to the essence of the psyche:

The Base of All Metaphysics

And now, gentlemen,
A word I give to remain in your memories and minds,
As base and finale too for all metaphysics.

(So to the students the old professor
At the close of his crowded course.)

Having studied the new and antique, the Greek and Germanic systems,
Kant having studied and stated, Fichte and Schelling and Hegel,
Stated the lore of Plato, and Socrates greater than Plato,
And greater than Socrates sought and stated, Christ divine having studied
    long,
I see reminiscent today those Greek and Germanic systems,
See the philosophies all, Christian churches and tenets see,

Yet underneath Socrates clearly see, and underneath Christ the divine I
    see,
The dear love of man for his comrade, the attraction of friend to friend,
Of the well-married husband and wife, of children and parents,
Of city for city and land for land.

                                              –Walt Whitman

To understand Jung's worldview and to speak the language of depth psychology, we first stumble onto the problem of defining terms for the indefinable and ambiguous...things that are not "things." Terms like "mind," "psyche," "soul," "spirit," and "Self" are not always clear or used consistently, even by Jung. Such terms can only be understood by association to the effects they have on us and the meanings we give them. In the next few chapters, we will review some meanings that speak to our experience of these words.

5

Defining Psyche, Soul, Mind, and Spirit

O the mind, mind has mountains, cliffs of fall
Frightful, sheer, no man-fathomed.
Hold them cheap
May who ne'er hung there.

– Gerard Manley Hopkins

The poet knows that one who explores the depths of the mind finds a glorious and terrifying universe. Our research chips away at those mountains and cliffs of fall, and each effort opens new questions.

Despite the fact that we live in a largely materialistic era, we still use the word "soul," though we would not all agree on its meaning. But "psyche" appears infrequently outside of the literature of the depth psychologists. There, "psyche" and "soul" are often used interchangeably (at least in English). In my experience, "psyche" often connotes the larger set/container and describes the totality of human experience, including that experience which is beyond the level of consciousness. In this way it differs from "mind," which suggests only conscious experience. "Psyche" includes all that is known and capable of being known, and it therefore can be pictured as existing throughout the universe as if it is a vast sea of energy.

In that sense, "soul" cannot be differentiated from "psyche," but "soul" is found to be used more often when speaking in an individual context; something more intimate than the vast psyche is conjured up. However, this is not always true, and sometimes the word "soul" implies the totality of experience, the equivalent of "psyche," as in soul of the world, Anima Mundi, and Universal Soul.

When we speak of experiencing soul or psyche, we are not limiting that to ideas, because "thinking ideas" is too narrow a definition for what human minds do; they also guess, intuit, wonder, imagine, plan, obsess, sense, dream, lie, anguish, rejoice, adore, imitate, and so on. There is an emotional or affective component to human mind along with its capacity to think logically. It is the affective component that makes a difference between the humans and the cyborgs in science-fiction. It is the factor that makes it impossible, so far, to replicate human thinking in robots, because humans bring an ability to prioritize, to sense subtle meanings and "read between the lines," to make ethical judgments.

The psyche is active whether we are conscious of it or not. In Jungian thought the psyche is universal and fathomless, and we as individuals participate in a larger group psyche or world soul, sometimes called the collective unconscious. In sleep and other unconscious states, as long as the body is alive, the psyche is active. While we have the impression that we direct our own inner experience most of the time, we must admit that some psychic experiences, like dreams or sudden insights, do impinge upon us involuntarily, as if from outside ourselves. Sometimes we remember what the psyche registered while we were unconscious, but usually not. In the same way, physical experiences (cellular functions, the action of inner organs, muscle spasms, etc.) move us involuntarily whether we are conscious of them or not.

Many discoveries and insights of philosophy, science, music, and creative inspirations seem to emerge from levels of the psyche so deep that we experience them as coming from outside of ourselves. Musicians tell us, "I heard the music and rushed to write it down before it disappeared." Writers say, "It was as if I was being given dictation and was not in control of what was emerging." There are levels of psyche that operate outside of space and time, as in visions which later come true in conscious time, and dreams when past and future events happen simultaneously.

Creative people find their creative process to be a cooperative joining of varying degrees of consciousness. There are many examples of problems solved during sleep and dreams. Physicist Lee Smolin describes how the second version of his theory of Doubly Special Relativity came to be:

> We were working in a café in uptown Waterloo called the Symposium, with comfortable couches. He (João Magueijo) was jetlagged. I was traumatized and exhausted, having just returned from a weekend in New York following the

events of September 11. I fell asleep as João was talking, then woke up to find him dozing. I remembered something he had said as I was losing consciousness, and I played with it on a pad, then fell asleep again. I woke up when he started talking, and we had a few mutually lucid minutes before he fell asleep again. And so the afternoon went, as we talked, calculated, and dozed in turn. I can only imagine what the café staff thought. But at some point during that afternoon, we hit on a key fact that had evaded us for months, having to do with trading moments for positions. When we were done we had invented a second version of DSR...(Smolin, *The Trouble with Physics*, p. 232.)

There seem to be two meanings for soul: sometimes it refers to the whole psyche, and sometimes a particular aspect of the psyche that has to do with connection and images of union. Jung sometimes spoke of soul as an agent of the Holy Spirit or Anima Mundi in an ongoing creation of the imaginal world. Without it, the world seems deadened and worthless.

When people are asked to draw the soul as they picture it, many different images emerge; birds, people with wings, eyes, and waves of radiation are a few. This human capacity called "soul" seems like an invisible psychological "organ," an inner eye or ear, whose function is to seek out experiences of relationship, connection, and unity. In poetic terms we might say the soul is the organ that is capable of perceiving the supernatural. In quasi-scientific terms we can imagine that it resonates to a vast psychoenergetic spectrum, which Jung thought could be compared with the electromagnetic spectrum. Perhaps this requires some explanation of Jung's understanding of psychic energy.

Jung was not a dualist in the tradition of believing in separation of mind and body. He believed that the same energy formed mind and body, and psychic energy existed on a continuum, like electromagnetic energy, which contains short and long energetic wavelengths. Theoretically, the long end of the electromagnetic spectrum, which we know as radio waves, stretches to the end of the universe. The gamma rays at the short end theoretically become smaller into infinity. Instinctual energy that moves us physically, like long infrared wavelengths, Jung imagined to be on the continuum towards one end of the pole; more ethereal or less dense energy that manifests in ideas or spiritual experiences veered toward the other pole, like the short wavelengths on the ultraviolet end of the electromagnetic spectrum. He believed that physics would someday discover the principle that would explain how matter and energy are one in terms that the human mind can comprehend. ("On the Nature of the Psyche," CW 8, par. 381-442.)

To define the soul by how we "know" it, we might say it is being open to the whole spectrum of experience, perceiving the value of all experience—bodily senses and instinctual drives as well as those experiences that can't be perceived through the senses. The soul is our function that allows us to imagine, feel, and conceive of things spiritual, all that transcends the limits of physicality. Transpersonal values, ethical attitudes, those intangibles that stir the heart, are the dealings of the soul. It is attracted to life and is not bound by space-time constraints. It contemplates living eternally in the present. Immortality cannot be proved, philosophically or empirically, but it is a universal idea acceptable to the soul. It is human to wonder about immortality and highly unusual not to consider it. The depth psychologist sees the importance and legitimacy of such ideas as normal elements of the psyche. To wonder about the unknown is built into us; it is not a pathological symptom as some skeptics see it.

Jung saw "soul" as the living thing in man that lures us into the inertness of matter and, by making us believe incredible things, pulls us into life. It animates matter. The soul knows the reality of visions and is a "spiritual faculty." So in everyday language, when a person scoffs at tenderness or at the incredible and imaginal world, we call them "soulless."

The soul is not limited to things sweet and pink. Its scope is all of life, the dark and light. By animating our mundane world with soul, we participate in continuous creation. Ordinary, everyday things, even unpleasant ones, become illuminated by the extraordinary when we are "soulful."

Trying to differentiate what we mean by soul and spirit is another brain teaser. In an attempt to glean what humans mean by soul and spirit from many centuries of information, we can speak of some recognizable qualities. The word "spirit" corresponds to "soul" as "yang" to "yin" in Eastern philosophy. Here are Jung's words:

> Spirit is something higher than intellect since it embraces the latter and includes feelings as well. It is a guiding principle of life that strives toward superhuman, shining

heights. Opposed to this yang principle is the dark, feminine, earthbound yin, whose emotionality and instinctual-
ity reach back into the depths of time and down into the
labyrinth of the physiological continuum. ("Commentary
on 'The Secret of the Golden Flower,'" CW 13, par. 7.)

Both spirit and soul originate in the depths of the human psyche.
Because they come from beyond our conscious awareness, we experience them as from beyond ourselves. Spirit especially feels as if it comes
from "outside" and is experienced as that which tries to lift us out of
matter, while the soul tries to connect to matter and physiological life.
These pulls, or tendencies, that we experience in relation to physical
matter have given us these images of the inner life being directed by
these two aspects of the same capacity to imagine, which we call soul
and spirit.

Early philosophers pictured the soul connecting body and spirit. The
energy of the soul tends toward connection—love, desire, Eros, which
implies the ability to reflect on and appreciate its object. The soul's love
for bodily expression gives life its vitality. The spirit's love for reaching beyond life drives us to create, to imagine immortality. These two
aspects of interiority are not so much opposites as companions. Soul
longs for spirit; it pulls spirit to us. The spirit longs to become embodied
and incarnate to have its creativity expressed. This has been the subject
of several movies, such as "Wings of Desire" by German director Wim
Wenders, about a spirit or angel who admires the human capacity for
love and longs to know desire.

There is a dangerous aspect to spirit, which feels like something
thrilling, but alien, coming from outside, whereas soul is interiority
and depth. Spirit is fascinating, not reflective. It often manifests in a
personality when a crossroad of life occurs or a big decision is called
for. Then it spontaneously rises out of the unconscious and can easily
be projected onto a wise, charismatic, or magical figure. It does not
question itself but can take us over and blind us with light and energy;
we become crazy and inflated if not grounded by soul. Both spirit and
soul are aspects of psyche, as psyche includes the whole experience of
consciousness and unconsciousness.

It is easy to see how Jung was tempted to associate gender with these
dichotomies, ascribing a feminine inner soul to lure man to reach deeper into himself, and a masculine inner spirit to lure woman to reach

deeper into herself. The myth of Psyche and Eros illustrates this. Psyche (soul) was the beautiful girl whose love captivated Eros, the God of Love (spirit). But she could not keep him earthbound and connected to her mortality. Their story is one of longing and persistence in devotion, until, through trials and adventures, including a trip to the underworld, they are united in love.

6

Self

A noiseless, patient spider,
I mark'd, where, on a little promontory, it stood, isolated;
Mark'd how, to explore the vacant, vast surrounding,
It launch'd forth filament, filament, filament, out of itself;
Ever unreeling them—ever tirelessly speeding them.

And you, O my Soul, where you stand,
Surrounded, detached, in measureless oceans of space,
Ceaselessly musing, venturing, throwing,—seeking the spheres to connect them;
Till the bridge you will need, be form'd—till the ductile anchor hold,
Till the gossamer thread you fling, catch somewhere, O my Soul.

–Walt Whitman

The poet compares himself to a patient spider, isolated in space, ready to fling his soul to some place where it can take hold like an anchor, and secure him. We can think of the Self as such a place that the soul imagines. From a psychological perspective it is a reassuring state of mind where we go to find equilibrium. From a transcendent perspective it is an Other of superior consciousness who guides us home and provides anchorage. Here we review a few of those who influenced Jung in this concept.

Heraclitus (535-475 BCE) anticipated much that Jung's psychology incorporates today. He taught that individual things were merely appearances, and reality was in constant flux, and that opposites are not stable but are likely to turn, or unite. He intuited a unifying principle as a kind of intelligence and lawfulness which he called "logos." He distinguished between "knowledge" and "understanding," a distinction important today in the era of artificial intelligence. Although he was refuted by later early philosophers, including Plato, his ideas now are consistent with scientific notions of energy. Jung owes him the term "enantiodromia," referring to the tendency for any extreme condition to turn toward its opposite. In the philosophy of Heraclitus, there are four dimensions, the fourth being time, as energy is always moving in time and space.

Unlike Heraclitus, Plato (427-348 BCE) imagined a dual world: the material world of particular things which we perceive through our senses, and the non-material world of perfect ideals or essences (called Forms) beyond the material, changeable, worldly things. Jung's idea of archetypes—universal patterns that motivate living beings—is often considered Platonic, but actually it is different. Jung conceived of psychic and physical energy as one (as shown above in his comparing psychic energy with the electromagnetic spectrum). We perceive energy in different states (like water and steam). The archetypes of Jung's imagination were both material and spiritual, neither good nor bad. They could be positive or negative influences, depending on how they were expressed by humans. They are not "ideas," but forces that actively participate in our physical life, moving us as ways of being, especially through the instincts.

Jung's ideas were more like those of Plato's student, Aristotle (384-322 BCE). Aristotle objected to Plato's notion of a dual world; he argued with his teacher that the world was an expression of union of form and matter. Aristotle also anticipated "individuation" by teaching that each thing contained within its material being its end or final form, as acorn contains oak.

Plotinus (205-270 CE) was a passionate believer in an infinite, transcendent All. A Roman, he belonged to a school of philosophy known as the Neo-Platonists that combined many schools of thought: Platonic, Aristotelian, Stoic, Pythagorean, and even some of Jewish, Christian, and Asian religions. The Neo-Platonists hoped to lessen the influence of Christianity, but their efforts were thwarted by the Roman emperor, Justinian, who closed their academies in 529. Plotinus taught that the All is pure potentiality; it is neither being nor non-being, beyond attributes. It does not create but emanates. Creation continues to unfold in stages from the perfect All to gradually lesser and lesser perfection, but all creation is good because it is emanation of the All. Plotinus is said to have said on his deathbed: "Strive to give back the divine in yourselves to the divine in the All." (Wikipedia.) This message seems to me an antecedent of the individuation process, as will become clearer as we develop the idea of Self.

Immanuel Kant (1724-1804) is usually cited as Jung's primary influence in epistemology: the belief that all we can know is our inner experience; that we cannot perceive an objective reality outside of our own minds; that everything we know is filtered through our inner world; that a knowledge of moral order is built into the human mind and is the central fact of life. The idea that an inherent structure of the mind exists (Kant's *a priori* categories) is reflected in Jung's concept of the unconscious as organized around archetypes, and Freud's inner structures of id, ego and superego.

Similar to Plotinus's philosophy is that of a philosopher whom Jung refers to frequently, Friedrich von Schelling (1775-1854) of the Naturphilosophie school of German Romanticism. He held that nature and spirit sprang from a common principle, the World Soul, which generated the realms of matter, living nature, and human consciousness. The laws governing the realms are analogous, and the universe is an organized whole of connected parts.

Von Schelling's view of the unconscious was a theme found throughout Romantic thought. Man, the beautiful animal, a creature like all creatures of nature, found himself linked to the intangible, invisible, teeming life of the universe in profound mystery. (Ellenberger, *The Discovery of the Unconscious,* pp. 199-215.)

Arthur Schopenhauer's (1788-1860) writing influenced Jung as a young student. Both were interested in Eastern religions, and Jung borrowed the term "individuation" from him. Schopenhauer believed that the world consisted of phenomena, called representations, moved by a universal and unconscious dynamic force which he called "will." Schopenhauer's emphasis on the will as a sexual drive links him more with Freud, but his influence on Jung's theory of the power of the collective unconscious to influence behavior through a single dynamic principle (will) is clear. Many philosophers have tried to overcome the split between the physical and the mental or spiritual that permeated Western thought. Schopenhauer (and Leibnitz) looked to Eastern philosophies, like Taoism, for approaches, as did Jung.

Carl Gustav Carus (1789-1869) and Eduard von Hartmann (early 1800s) come up frequently in Jung's references. They both transposed Schopenhauer's "will" to "unconscious" and contributed greatly to the understanding of the role of the unconscious as it silently influences us in all aspects of life.

The All, the World Soul, the Will, the Unconscious—Jung saw in all of these the image of a principle of unity as a ground of being, which often is how people see their god. Remember that he insisted he was not describing a supernatural being, God, but the image of God that resides in the human imagination and flows from a central core of the psyche.

This superficial list by no means exhausts philosophical influences on Jung. We have not covered his debt to Asian philosophies, the Hebrew Kabbalah, the Gnostics, the alchemists, Hegel, Nietzsche, and others. Hegel's "Absolute" and Nietzsche's "Übermensche" are related to Jung's "Self." I am excluding discussing these influences because there is no way to describe the extent of debatable complications about Jung's relationships with these figures in the limits of this work. Later we will explore some comparisons with Buddhism. (Additional references are suggested in Part III, "Lagniappe.")

What is important here is that the concept of an all-pervasive World Soul, or principle of union, is the common factor in the philosophers that Jung respected. He saw that the human psyche produces—from some deep "layer"—the idea that an encompassing presence of unification exists beyond our human limitations. This observation led him to the idea that at the fundamental bedrock of the psyche is a desire for completion, purpose, and total fulfillment of potential, which he attributed to the Self.

We can focus on the Self as a container for all psychic forces and also a core of psychic energy. We repeatedly read that the Self can neither be defined nor understood intellectually, but must be experienced and known through its effect on us. The Self can be thought of as an ever-ongoing process which expresses itself in the human psyche as an urge to become an integrated being. It produces images of completion, unity, God. Sometimes we may attribute or project the energy carried by the Self onto another person, an entity, an institution, state, or any number of things that capture the imagination with a promise of union and completion, so that the object of that projection is given god-like status (e.g., Land of Liberty, Alma Mater, der Führer, Mother Nature).

I find it impossible to say how the Self differs from psyche, because when we leave the realm of psyche, we are no longer within human

capacity for the imaginal. If we can conceive of something more comprehensive than psyche, so that the psyche is contained within it along
with whatever can exist outside of psyche, that is Self. Every culture has
had its way of imagining the First Principle, the All, the One, and the
many names of God that reflect the human need to identify a container
and ordering principle for the universe. Because it is the source of all
psychic energy, it is our container as well as the force that puts our creativity into motion, according to Jung.

Our conscious awareness is contained in the ego complex, which is
only part of the psyche. The Self, being timeless, is conceived as con-
taining the ego and much more, including all that is knowable, and
unknowable, including the collective unconscious.

The Self may be represented by any number of things that we perceive as being a greater totality than our individual selves, and so will
appear differently to different personalities and in different cultures.
Though we may be inclined to think of the Self as an entity or being, we
cannot perceive the nature of the Self through our narrow windows of
perception and human reason. We can recognize its influence through
symbols that attract and provoke us. In the presence of Self symbols
we may feel overpowered by awe, love, humility, and gratitude or by
guilt, anxiety, and dread; heaven and hell are common symbols that
reflect these responses. When Jung says that the Self contains the All,
he means all possibilities, whether we perceive them as good or evil.

Some followers of Jung sense that by focusing on the unity of the
Self, we risk creating the notion of a particular God-image, or monothe-
ism. In doing so we would dismiss the complexity of the psyche and
run the danger of becoming too rigid and structured in our worldview,
but also in our evaluation of human behavior. Each God-image creates
its own worldview, with values and prejudices that can turn critical of
others. The view of one group of Jungians, the Archetypal Psychologists, provides a correction and warning that we must not become smug
or dogmatic about the rightness of our worldview, treatment methods,
and perceptions of pathology and health. We need to "honor all the
gods." Instead of focusing on a singular drive to become a personality
that is static, consistent and permanent, we could imagine a continually moving self-image influenced by changing archetypes and changing purposes. We could imagine the individuation process as moving,
not in a linear way, but in a spiral, circular, or random fashion. We can

describe this process as "mercurial individuation," that is, without an obvious preordained goal. "Mercurial" implies unpredictable and non-linear, whereas focus on the Self as a principle of order can bring up images of a monotheistic God, patriarchal, masculine, and intolerant.

Essential to this discussion is the understanding that symbols representing individuation and the Self are not consciously worked out by design. They *appear.* And they are universal only in their occurrence, not in their content. They are communications, representations from the collective unconscious, and as such, are personal and "numinous"—a word meaning "intensely awe-inspiring" which Jung used frequently. These messages from the collective unconscious cannot be objectified, quantified, or prescribed. Do we all receive them? Probably. Do we all pay attention to them? Probably not.

Dylan Thomas wrote a wonderful poem, "Ears in the Turret Hear" about making the choice to listen to invitations from life, or to close ourselves away out of fear. Here are the last few lines:

> Shall I let in the stranger, shall I welcome the sailor,
> Or stay till the day I die?
> Hands of the stranger and holds of the ships,
> Hold you poison or grapes?

We are not puppets buffeted around by chemicals in brain and body; we are persons with soul, will, and purposeful direction available to us. Although we are limited by our biology, heredity, and history, we are also strongly influenced by our intentions and sense of direction.

• • •

Homer's story of Odysseus (or Ulysses) can be read as a metaphor for the individuation process. Odysseus leaves his wife, Penelope, on a many-years' journey full of adventure, gore, and hubris. He begins as a proud heroic warrior and becomes a man of humility, wisdom, and peace aided by his relationship with the god Hermes, guide of the journey. During this long separation, both Odysseus and Penelope evolve into more fully conscious people who have realized their potentials and their capacity for the deep relationship that they come to find in their marital reunion. The story illustrates how husband and wife transform their ordinary marriage and themselves into a sacred union of masculine and feminine principles. In Chapter 15 we will compare this illustration of the individuation process with that of a modern example in James Joyce's *Ulysses*.

7

A Brief History of Individuation

*God has shown me the right choice, but my demons have me
tied to a spit and the fire has been lit.*

–Joseph Duncan, pedophile and murderer
Time magazine, July 18, 2005

Joseph Duncan appears to have a conscience, but he feels he has no choice in the life he leads. Is he conscious? How do we understand the choices we make, the paths we take? While some might agree with Duncan that he is possessed by demons, Jungians see this as the inability of his ego to withstand deep unconscious complexes which contain more psychic energy than is available to his conscious mind. But for all practical purposes, they may be thought of as demons.

Recently there have been several unrelated cases of a Chinese adult bursting into a school to slash with a knife or kill little children. Attempts to explain this frightening behavior usually focus on the factors that cause the perpetrators to be irrational, such as their plight in life that has left them hopeless and angry. But to understand why they chose the target of small children, we must go deep into unconscious motives. No ordinary interview can reveal such horrors. Only depth psychology can divulge their reasons, which are probably unconscious to them.

It is as if our minds are influenced by other unseen minds. Paradoxically, we each experience our own soul as individual and discrete, yet it is inseparable from the psyche of all other psychological beings, a collection which at this point in our knowledge cannot be defined. This paradox can be compared to the nature of light, whose every particle functions alone, and also as a collective wave. Duncan has trouble eliciting the empathic aspects of psyche, and many of us have trouble accessing the sadistic aspects which flourish in him.

Who participates in this collective psyche? Does psyche include animal and inanimate creation as participants in some level of consciousness? Popular opinion holds that the size of the brain determines who is conscious. A mosquito can only react at the level of a machine that switches on when conditions that stimulate a response reach a certain threshold, but a dog reacts at a more abstract level of interpreting gestures, words, and emotional tones. Accordingly, to some philosophers, the dog is more conscious and therefore has a soul, but the mosquito does not. (Hofstadter, *I Am a Strange Loop*, p. 190.) But neuropsychologist Antonio Damasio warns against using size of brain areas as an index of power or energy of mental faculties. It is not that simple. (Damasio, *Descartes' Error*, p. 16.)

Jung told a story about this question. When he was small the cook killed a cock, took it to Jung's mother in the kitchen and told her that the cock died "asking forgiveness like a Christian, so he will go to heaven." Jung's mother argued that chickens did not have an immortal soul and did not go to heaven. The cook insisted that there is a chicken heaven, and that all animals have a heaven, because when the Savior came down to earth, the animal Savior came to the animals, so they can repent their sins in order to go to heaven. Jung comments that the cook's theology represents the "mentality which saw the drama of redemption going on at all levels and could therefore discover it even in the mysterious and incomprehensible transformation of matter." ("Religious Ideas in Alchemy," CW 12, par. 495.)

The field of animal cognition, animal intelligence, and animal communication is growing rapidly. Mainly we are separated from knowing how animals think through language barriers, and when psychologists are able to teach animals our language, we find that their capacities for concept formation are greater than was suspected in previous times.

Creatures of all eons, those barely distinguishable from inorganic matter, the simple protoplasms, the crustaceans which are as much minerals as animals, the cold-blooded reptiles, the hot-blooded hunters, the warm-blooded mammals, the indifferent predators and loving nurturers—all are contained in the human psyche. Sometimes they become obvious when through illness, drugs, or accident the structures of the civilized brain of the frontal cortex are inhibited and nonfunctional. Or we dream.

> The animal soul in man...extends downward through a
> level containing the berserker specters of humanity's past
> epochs, and thence, as Jung puts it, down to the animal
> souls of Pithecanthropus and the hominids; next to the
> "psyche" of the cold-blooded saurians, and finally, deepest
> of all, to the transcendental mystery and paradox of the
> sympathetic and parasympathetic psychoid processes....
> These elements, qualities, and symbolic animals are pre-
> figurations and carriers of the self. The structure of whole-
> ness is present but deeply buried in the unconscious. It can
> always be found if one risks oneself by attaining the widest
> and deepest range of consciousness, but it requires a self-
> knowledge and reflective attitude that consists of project-
> ing oneself into the empirical self as it really is, and not
> into forms, rituals, games, dares, or into the "self" as we
> like to think we are. (Grinnell, *Alchemy in a Modern Woman*,
> p. 89.)

Comparing a mosquito, which functions minimally on its own, with a robot, which plays chess through the directions programmed by a human, opens more complicated issues. People become very attached to robots that are programmed to respond to touch and voice, and easily project soulful qualities onto them. Anyone who has loved an animal finds it easy to imagine that a soul exists there. Buddhists draw the soul boundary at the level of sentient beings. Pantheists imagine the divine soul present in all matter, including rocks, wind, and rivers. Paradox, mystery, and uncertainty is the territory of psychology, the study of soul.

The notion of an individual soul must have always existed in a vague way. We suspect this because the sense of soul is reflected in the importance placed on burial ceremonies by early humans. Why would people struggling for survival go to the trouble of honoring the bodies of the dead with such care and rituals? It must be that they saw life as something sacred, to be respected. Perhaps they hoped it would regenerate, like a seed. It appears that the clear awareness of the individual soul evolved slowly as civilization and religion advanced. Soul may have been attributed to the tribe or family for survival purposes. We know that kings, priests, and medicine men acted as conduits for divine messages and can be seen as representatives of the soul for the group. That would have discouraged listening to one's own soul-stirrings.

A recent story in the news told of a Pakistani woman who at age fourteen was given in marriage to an old man. Although some women choose to leave such marriages when they are offered the opportunity to do so by groups who dedicate themselves to freeing marital prisoners, this woman dared not disappoint her parents and refused to leave. The bonds that stress the importance of tribal survival are more important to that family than are individual rights.

Yet the seed of the individuation process has been with us at the very least since the Greek civilization recognized individual worth (though less so the individual worth of slaves or women). The first known systematized promotion of human personality development known to Western civilization is that of Pythagoras. This early philosopher attracted followers who believed that the universe consisted of a mathematical relationship between all things, culminating in a harmonious balance. Within this system each individual had the responsibility to find his or her own balance, to develop his or her soul so as to perfectly fit into the harmony of the universe and contribute to its mathematical and musical perfection. As you see, this is very much like Jung's idea that the consciousness of the individual contributes to the collective knowledge available to future generations. However, there is an important difference in the Pythagorean development toward "perfection" and Jung's idea of "completion," which we will see later.

The Pythagoreans' proposed way of perfecting oneself involved following rituals and traditions, such as entering the temples barefoot; worshipping the gods; attending to burial of the dead; memorizing and handing down maxims; practicing silence; and following dietary restrictions whose details are no longer accessible to us.

To illustrate the notion that all knowledge is present in the collective consciousness, we can look at the current interest in sound waves in the universe that tell us a lot about our earth's beginnings. We can also consider the suggestion from string theory that vibrations create matter in the form of particles called phonons. These theories that preoccupy physicists with sound continue to reverberate with the intuitions of Pythagoras.

For example, the physicist Lee Smolin writes:

> A string has overtones, just like a piano string or a guitar string, and natural numbers denote the various levels of vibration.... There is a wave associated with every particle...

> and a particle associated with every wave, including a particle associated with the sound wave traveling through the metal. It is called a phonon... it has mass, momentum, it carries energy... We say that a phonon is an "emergent particle." (Smolin, *The Trouble with Physics*, p. 131-132.)

New technologies have enabled us to detect gravity waves which surge through the cosmos, adding an auditory dimension to the images we study about the fabric of space-time, and connecting us with the rhythm of the universe. (See Bartusiak on this subject.)

The Pythagoreans' notion of the point or monad was a projection of the notion of divine unity, the origin of geometry and of the earth. Their symbol of the tetractys, the first four numbers, which contain the basic musical intervals, the fourth, fifth, and octave, and their three principles (one becomes two, two become three, and out of the third comes the one, or fourth), relate intuitively to the three stages of union in the process of individuation. (Edinger, *The Mysterium Lectures*.) In Chapter 9 we will look at these stages of union in individuation.

Individual psychological development was not known to be of interest as nation states, tribes, empires, and hordes vied for power. A significant event in Western history, the signing of the Magna Carta in the thirteenth century, reflected the beginning of a change in focus from power at the top to consideration for the rights of lesser men. By the eighteenth century, influenced by the diminishing power of the monarchies, the rise of industry and the flourishing of the sciences, the individual began to consider civil rights. In each era there were always gifted individuals who envisioned or displayed great awareness of the psyche, particularly among European Romanticists and American Transcendentalists. But only after medicine progressed to a point of considering mental illness a treatable problem could the study of the psyche evolve, thanks largely to the French medical schools and their interest in hypnosis. We might say that until the birth of depth psychology, individuation took place naturally and without benefit of conscious attention. Spiritual disciplines preceded it and flourished in the East.

Many programs of self-development followed those of Pythagoras, but few of them encouraged a personal journey that did not depend on conforming to some collective system or belief. Jung was one of few voices encouraging us to listen to our own souls and not to rely on collective authority to do our soul-work for us. It is still the case that Jung's message, unlike other "self or spiritual growth" programs, does not depend on following another soul's way. At Jung's funeral the minister referred to him as a prophet who had, in a time of rationalism, given man the courage to have a soul again. (Ellenberger, *The Discovery of the Unconscious*, p. 678.)

8

Two Ways of Individuating

Jolande Jacobi's classic description of individuation maintains that there are two types of individuation with any number of intermediate stages. Those types are: the natural process, which occurs without the participation of consciousness, and the "artificial" process, aided by definite methods—including Jungian psychoanalysis—and consciously experienced. I prefer to call this second way the "*reflective* individuation process."

FIRST WAY: According to Jacobi, the majority of us follow the unconscious, natural path unreflectively, curtailing our individual development in order to avoid hardship; we stop short of being true to ourselves by imitating others, maintaining an identity with a group, and trying to avoid catastrophe. This means that most of us are seeking development to a point but willing to stop and fall in with a group norm when being outside the norm becomes too lonely and uncomfortable.

Even so, Jacobi says, there are those who follow the natural path and attain wisdom and wholeness, living consciously either through hard-won discipline or through "individuation granted them even in the cradle, as a gift of grace." Examples she gives are the tribal medicine man or wise man/woman, the saint, the hero, dedicated philosopher, scientist, artist... all who do not seek happiness via the path of least resistance, but are moved to live beyond popular conventions in order to fulfill some purpose. But living beyond conventions and being dedicated to a cause does not necessarily describe individuation. One might ask why we do not include the outlaw in this group. In Part II, Chapter 16, we will take up the question of exceptional people.

Many unsung ordinary people acquire amazing levels of consciousness and integration without overt assistance. The way may be blocked by any number of problems, such as psychosis, substance abuse, premature interruptions of sickness or disaster. In cases of short life, Jacobi says we must distinguish between a life lived to the full or broken off as incomplete.

SECOND WAY: All of us do a certain amount of imitation of parents and others in our growing years, but there comes a point when we begin to see what's right for us, what we hold dear. Even though those values change, even though we can play many roles and put on many different personas or masks, we begin to have a sense of continuity of personality, and some of us seriously search for integrity. Jung described the second way as an *opus contra naturam*, or "a work against nature" (a term borrowed from alchemists). In this way we deliberately shape our behavior in consultation with the Self. It demands an effort. We must pay attention to the unconscious messages and content as we find them in night dreams, day dreams, hunches, accidents, talents, and inspirations. Not only do we listen to these messages, but we have to evaluate them ethically. We take responsibility for everything we do; we make each decision and action in reflection upon its ethical context, in the interests of discovering what is singular or unique to the integrity of our personality. This way also is threatened by the same problems besetting the natural process: psychosis, substance abuse, sickness, and disaster. But ideally, the deliberately reflective person has the option to struggle through the obstacles and meet them head-on with a sense of support from the Self, and to place them in the fabric of his or her whole life, finding meaning or redemption in suffering through them, rather than being overcome by them.

This differentiation of two types of individuation sounds straightforward enough, but what of the "intermediate stages"? Few of us are able to sustain such consistent self-awareness as described in the second way, yet numerous people are searching for growth and are willing to follow various and often strange methods and leaders in the hope of "self-fulfillment" or "personal growth," a condition which cannot be described simply as happiness. It is not easy to find a helpful guide or companion in the work if we are motivated to grow but can't afford the time and money to be in analysis.

Psychology's purpose is to make us aware of the soul. All else is irrelevant in the grand scheme of things... neither success, nor health, nor even happiness, but the finding of a place where the soul rests and is satisfied, even if it is a difficult place. What does my soul want?

The question, "Who is able to carry through with this process?" opens a large and potentially contentious debate, which the later chapter on elitism will flesh out. For now, we will keep in mind that in order to follow Jung's reflective way of individuation, certain requirements must be met:

First, a capacity for reflection—or what academic psychology calls "an observing ego"; that means you must be emotionally stable enough to stand back and watch yourself and even criticize your own behavior when it is inappropriate. You can pause and think before you react, or at least, soon after!

Then you must be in a relationship with another person who also has some capacity for reflection *and* dialogue, who can help you in the struggle with confusing issues because they have dealt with the issues in their own life. Ideally this would be a trained analyst, who can see the archetypal reflections in your behavior. Alternatively a consciously evolved mentor or confidante can help.

Also, you must have enough energy to sustain the effort and the intention to seek consciousness.

Finally, a spoonful of humility is required. Arrogance must be left at the threshold.

• • •

No matter how long we work at this, there is always more openness to be gained. Even a person who has analyzed for a long time may have to push himself to confront a disagreement or avoid taking a cowardly way out of a jam or unpleasant task. Psychoanalysts often go back into analysis to work on difficult issues.

Reflective individuation is possible without a trained therapist under the right circumstances, but working with a Jungian psychoanalyst is most reliably helpful, provided that person is well-trained in the work. In choosing any psychotherapist, it is important to know whether they have been in long-term psychodynamic psychotherapy themselves. Ask them. If individuation is your soul-work, seeking out one who has studied it is like finding the mentor, such as Zen master, guru, graduate school professor, or master artist in any field whom you can trust with your soul.

For several years there has been a bias against long-term (more than one year) psychodynamic psychotherapy in favor of short-term (several months at most), goal-oriented therapies, including Behavioral, Cognitive-Behavioral, Hypnotherapy, Experience Based, Medication

Based therapies, etc. The purpose of short-term therapies, which are promoted by insurance companies, is to solve specific problems. They can be life-saving and beneficial, both in the short and in the long run. But only recently have we begun to collect data which shows that for people with multiple diagnoses (that includes most of us), as well as those who are looking for permanent character change and overall life-satisfaction, long-term psychodynamic psychotherapy is more effective than any others. (See Part III for references to these studies.)

If Jungian psychoanalysis is not needed or not available, there is group study. Meeting regularly with like-minded others who are curious about the reality of the psyche, particularly, if possible, with an analytically trained leader, is one way of furthering the reflective and unending individuation process.

> *I live my life in growing orbits*
> *which move out over the things of the world.*
> *Perhaps I can never achieve the last,*
> *but that will be my attempt.*
>
> *I am circling around God, around the ancient tower,*
> *and I have been circling for a thousand years,*
> *and I still don't know if I am a falcon, or a storm,*
> *or a great song.*

–Rainer Maria Rilke
Selected Poems of Rainer Maria Rilke

Part II

Individuation in the Twenty-First Century

9

The Opus: Finding the Spirit in Matter

We must each follow an individual path, but the paths have some things in common. Jung's three stages of individuation are still relevant (CW 14). We just have to be careful to not adopt a slavish attitude about stages. (See Chapter 15.) While some movement requires a starting point and proceeds from simplicity into more complexity and differentiation, some movement appears to move randomly back and forth between "stages." In order to describe an increase in conscious awareness, we need to look at the state of consciousness that we begin with. This will differ in each person, but in general, we begin with a sacrifice.

While on one hand individuation is a natural process, on the other hand, Jung describes it in the Latin term as the *"opus contra naturam,"* the "work against nature." In some respects we go against our nature to find our authentic being. At the same time, Jung says that the process cannot be accomplished without 1) including the needs of the instinctual body and 2) being in relationship to another human being. He is very clear that this is not a purely spiritual quest which takes us out of contact with the world into some heady stratosphere. It is a down-to-earth process.

FIRST STAGE: We begin with a natural state in which body, soul, and spirit are united unconsciously. The first move is to awaken the soul, to acknowledge the reality of the soul, to intend to pay attention to it. Then begins the psychological equivalent of disrobing. That means that we have to assume an attitude of openness, clearly looking at ourselves without pretense or disguise of any kind. We must decide that we will be brutally honest in our self-examination. If we go to a physician or a psychotherapist, we should not try to make a good impression or create a phony persona. We want the doctor or therapist to be able to see the real person and be better able to treat the real problem. So, when we go to meet the Other, the unconscious, we go without pretense.

In the individuation process, the next step is to look at the actual disrobed body and ask it to allow the inner work of attending to the soul and spirit. Even though the body and its relationships with others are essential parts of the process, in the beginning we attempt to overcome the body's demand for attention. Denying the body means that self-discipline, the ability to stand back from one's desires, is necessary in the beginning. The analogy here is "preparing the vessel" as we refine the body which houses the soul. The metaphor of self-discipline is found in numerous stories of fulfilling one's destiny; for example, the wild bull must be tamed by the god Mithra, the knight must kill his dragon, Plato's charioteer/soul must rein in his wild horses, et cetera.

This is the "first stage" (*unio mentalis*), and it will vary in difficulty from person to person. For example, for the person addicted to substances, this step is very difficult. In order to speak without interference with the Self through its manifestation in the unconscious, the compulsive attachment to particular drugs, foods, and behaviors must be addressed. For this reason psychoanalysis cannot begin until the subject has taken responsibility for his or her addiction. Addiction is like a false and demanding God or Self with a goal of its own; it will not allow free choices to be made, as anyone knows who has tried to maintain a relationship while having to answer to a compulsion for alcohol, drugs, sex, food, gambling, and so on. The desire for the drug will always come first, no matter how much you want to be a good partner or friend. Addictions function like demons, which used to be considered entities that would take possession of us. Now we understand them as mind-altering habits, or physiological patterns of reward, but we still cannot allow them to control our lives.

This does not mean that a person with an addiction is in any way less capable of being individuated. An addiction can be a tremendous catalyst for individuation. Jung's contribution to the "Big Book" of Alcoholics Anonymous stresses the spiritual potential expressed by an addiction. What is implied by this stage is that addictions be treated consciously.

We cannot judge the extent to which another person deals with their demons. It is very tempting to judge those who have virtually committed suicide too early in life through addiction — Dylan Thomas, Charlie Parker, Elvis Presley, Kurt Cobain, Theodore Rothko, Judy Garland, Jackson Pollock, Michael Jackson, the list goes on — and ask if they cheated themselves and the world by refusing to individuate. But we must not judge. We simply do not know how much they became themselves because of or despite their addictions. Neither can we see what goes on within a person in their attempt to deal with an addiction. It is said that true talent does not come about through addiction, but in spite of it; but that statement cannot be demonstrated. Those who continue to struggle with addictions and survive know something about individuation that is not universally known.

Besides becoming aware of addiction, the individuation process begins with being willing to put aside physical comforts to a certain extent in order to hear the demands of the immaterial or spiritual needs of the soul. This means that when one is called to develop a new attitude or new level of awareness, the discomfort following that change needs to be permitted. A simple example: if an adult who lives dependently with his parents follows a call to become independent, he may face a degree of deprivation. He will suffer the discipline of going to work, having less access to comforts, and so on. Most new attitudes require a period of sacrifice of physical comfort, and one must be willing to accept that as the first stage of individuation. This may require giving up a sexual relationship, facing punishment, sacrificing money for entertainment and luxuries, sleeping less, giving up a secure marriage, or other such accommodations.

Sometimes individuation requires us to get up and move out into the world in some way that we have avoided. Social anxiety may have to be contended with. Phobias and obsessions have to be addressed. Job hunting, dating, moving, public speaking, and other disagreeable tasks may be needed. But often this stage requires being alone to some degree, and withdrawing from whatever gives us comfort in order to hear the quiet voice of the soul. Fairy tales, which are often about the individuation process of the protagonist, usually include a period in the protagonist's development when he or she has to be alone, lost or withdrawn or imprisoned or journeying. This is when the inner direction begins to take place, the move that will allow him or her to seize an opportunity and make a choice. Loneliness is a universal experience, and each one of us must learn how to comfort and enjoy ourselves by ourselves. It is not that we need to seek out loneliness, but we must manage it when it is our fate.

Consciousness can be isolating, not only because of becoming more choosy about how we spend our time, but because others who are less conscious may be made uncomfortable and attack or ostracize us in a "scapegoat" attitude. For example, the designated patient in a family system is sometimes the one who is most aware of the unspoken problems and cannot fit in with the system. He or she is seen as abnormal, when often he/she is the one who is reacting most naturally to a dysfunctional family system.

Sometimes the individuation process requires that a relationship with the Self takes priority over a relationship with a therapist if it appears that the therapist does not support individuation. If your therapist does not encourage a path of consciousness, you may have to find another therapist. I have known several people who may have postponed their own growth when their therapists advised them to stay in abusive or self-constricting situations because they (the patient) would lose money or status by leaving.

Individuation involves becoming aware of the influences that keep us following patterns of behavior that are not adaptive. Patterns that are habitual, involuntary, and not subject to the ego's best judgment are called "complexes." They drive us by means of unconscious motives, until we uncover the underlying experiences that are being expressed. It is part of the first stage of individuation to learn to see what is behind our complexes, things such as early experiences, maladaptive attachments, unrealistic ideas, and impulsive tendencies. By stopping and reflecting before reacting in our typical ways, we exchange some spontaneity for mindfulness.

We all suffer from unconscious complexes. We ruin our marriages by unknowingly treating our spouses as we felt toward our hated sisters or brothers or mother, etc. We deny ourselves opportunities because we respond to our employers or teachers as we did to an arrogant parent. We fail to communicate our ideas because we present them from an old attitude of inferiority and apology, or fanaticism. We drive away our spouses, colleagues, and children with our unconscious need to feel superior, and we never learn what happened. We die before our time because we forgive ourselves our excessive appetites, deny their effects, and dismiss our symptoms as insignificant. We cannot escape these human frailties without concentrated effort and the help of another understanding person to keep us on track. Because of unconscious complexes, wonderfully intelligent philosophers can see through to the essence of life and still live miserable lives; psychologists can teach us how to understand human nature yet fail to be loved by their own children; beautiful women can have dozens of admirers but fail to find love. Individuation does not mean we have no more complexes to deal with, for complexes are the structure of our psyches; it means we have learned to see and resist acting impulsively out of complexes.

The journey of individuation is "slow cooking," not the instant effect we have come to expect from fast-foods and instant messaging. All the ingredients of a mindful life, its basic ingredients and its spices, need to simmer and come together gradually for a good result. In the same way, to understand and untangle our complexes and to face our character faults and inferiorities, then bring our lives together again, is a long, slow process, painful and disappointing at times.

The thing that makes Jung's approach unique is that he taught us to value the help that we get, not just from the analyst or our allies in the exterior life, but from the inner resources given to us by the millions of years of experience of those who survived before us. Within the deep caverns of the soul is information and inspiration to aid us on our journey. We have only to want it, ask for it, and listen to find it. Wanting it takes persistence. Asking for it takes humility. Listening means paying attention to what nature has to tell us, and also listening to dreams, coincidences, and informants from the past who come to us as geniuses of art, music, thought, medicine, and spirituality. In whatever form these informants present themselves, call them representatives of the Self. They may, for example, be personalities that speak to us, or opportunities, or images of physical reality that show us how our world is constituted, or poetic, artistic, or musical themes that come to us from another dimension.

SECOND STAGE: In the second stage of individuation, after we have opened up our awareness through self-examination and have gone deeply enough into our unconscious to not only uncover our unreasonableness, but to face it and deal with it, we now find and bring up our creative energy. This takes time, not the eight or ten sessions allowed by "managed care" insurance companies for psychotherapy to help.

There is no timetable to tell us when we are ready to move back into spontaneity and reconnect with the demands of the body. It happens when we are confident about what we want to be and express, because we know who we are, and we can count on ourselves not to betray our deepest core values. We can enjoy our instincts, not be compelled by them. This is the nature of the "second stage" that Jung described, in which we return soul and spirit to union with body and allow legitimate physical needs to assert themselves. In other words, we do not become masochistic in our interest in listening to the inner directions, nor do we withdraw from active participation in the world. We have come to know that our ego's view of life is not the whole picture. There is another center of consciousness that gives us a larger perspective on life; that is the point of view of the Self in which we dwell without being in control. When we become comfortable trusting in the Self instead of our own plans for ourselves, we can participate in life with our full being. We have learned by reflection to integrate thought and feeling. We have had enough experience through mistakes and humiliation to know our shortcomings, and enough success to believe in our abilities. We have had enough insights into our notions of right and wrong to have a sturdy value system, and we know what we would live for or die for.

The second stage of individuation is the goal of psychoanalysis in its popular meaning. It describes fully developed individuals who, though no one can ever become completely aware of the unconscious—which as far as we can tell is infinite—know themselves, are reasonably satisfied with who they have become, and rest in the presence of the Self as within a supportive cushion. In paragraphs 705-706 of CW 14, "The Conjunction," Jung describes his method of "active imagination" as a way of coming to that knowledge of Self by deliberately calling up images from the unconscious to interact with. (See Part III, "Lagniappe," Chapter 9.)

In the second stage we have learned the habit of reflecting on our perceptions and behavior, expressing ourselves to a degree that gives us fulfillment, and checking ourselves against the reality of others in our environment to be sure we are not entirely self-oriented and self-absorbed. We are aware of our inner divisiveness, our evil nature as well as our good, and we can look our hates and our loves squarely in the face without backing away. We may have evolved to a point where we can even make significant contributions to society. We are likely to be contented with our lot a good bit of the time and are humble enough to feel grateful about it. We also acknowledge that individuation is never complete; we may need help from time to time and are able to consult others or even go back into analysis or therapy if necessary.

As Jungian psychoanalyst Lawrence Alschuler says, "self-awareness marks the second stage of individuation, while awareness of powers in the psyche greater than oneself marks stage three." (Lawrence Alschuler in *The Cambridge Companion to Jung,* Young-Eisendrath and Dawson, eds., p. 282.)

THIRD STAGE: The third stage of individuation is marked by the experience of transcendence and a conviction that a unity of soul contains all of existence. It also divides the field of Jungian psychology theoretically into those who experience transcendence as something holy and sacred, a relationship with divinity, and those who experience transcendence as a high state of awareness without implying spiritual meaning. Jung called it the stage of the "unus mundus," or one world. Jung described it as being able to "unite the opposites," a phrase which is confusing and meaningless to a younger generation which has not usually experienced a world of clearly defined opposites. He also described it as "self-knowledge." He devotes the last chapter of his last book, *Mysterium Coniunctionis*, to these unions or conjunctions.

This last stage of individuation can best be explained by saying that having attained a level of comfort in ourselves and immediate surroundings, in the third stage we see the world as one body. We feel grateful for being part of it, and we want to give something back to a world which has immediacy and intimacy. We are not satisfied to feel grateful; we also want to express and acknowledge the fact. There is a need to express a sense of sacredness and gratitude in an experience of union with the All.

> The complications arising at this stage are no longer egotistic wish-conflicts, but difficulties that concern others as much as oneself. ("The Relations Between the Ego and the Unconscious," CW 7, par. 275.)

After we have become accustomed to consulting with the inner sources, voices, or figures representing the Self, we come to experience the essence of our relationship with the larger consciousness. Although hate and the subjective experience of evil are never fully transcended in the finite world, that intimate relationship to the Self can only be motivated by love; that is the paradoxical nature of the third coniunctio.

When we have asked for and received a connection to the Self, we experience this as a mutual attraction, being with a lover, as the poetry of mystics and the biblical Song of Songs expresses. Hostility or indifference would result in an absence of connection. But this connection is experienced as real, a real connection as one with the universe. When Einstein said that the essential human question is, "Is the universe friendly?" he must have intuited this possibility. To those who would see spirituality as irrational, I would say that some are strongly moved to contemplate and worship life and the giver of life, and to enjoy a feeling of gratitude for having been allowed to experience life, even when it does not make rational sense.

> The only work remaining at this stage is to know the million faces of God as they reveal themselves in the imaginative realm, and to deepen forever the bonds of relationship and love that joins ego and self. Moreover, the human being has become the "man of paradise" for with the attainment of the third level of union we find ourselves in paradise, for paradise is where the light of God shines without hindrance. The paradise of the soul is within, and the soul participates in that reality, whatever else is occurring in the outside world. (Raff, *Jung and the Alchemical Imagination*, p. 248.)

There is yet another dimension of psychological being, beyond the experience of Other, when all separateness dissolves into No-thing and becomes the state of the soul absorbed in union. Some have been able to identify this psychic state beyond the archetypal, a state corresponding to the image of Stillness which precedes the urgency to create. It cannot be described, except by silence. It is not amenable to a psychology that has the objective of observing something. It is amenable to poetry, mysticism, art, dance, and music.

> *There is a flag that no one sees blowing in the sky-temple.*
> *A blue cloth has been stretched up,*
> *it is decorated with the moon and many jewels.*
>
> *The sun and the moon can be seen in that place;*
> *when looking at that, bring your mind down to silence.*

I will tell you the truth:
the person who has drunk from that liquid wanders around
like someone insane.

–Kabir
quoted in Bly, *The Kabir Book*

10

Inner and Outer

Is individuation too solitary and introspective? It is in the interaction of the individual and the collective world that we find the greatest misunderstandings about Jung's psychology. Individuation is not a retreat into thinking, but an opening and welcoming of all of life.

Jung's process of individuation has been criticized by some who note that its emphasis on personality growth suggests that we are not concerned with the world of social issues and communities. Although that was not Jung's intention—he was very much a worldly man and very much aware of the larger common interests—the criticism has been true for some. In an effort to stress the importance of introversion in a world that does not value the inner, contemplative style, undoubtedly Jungians have sometimes created the opposite bias. Here I would like to clarify that the objective of individuation assumes that individuals functioning at their most fulfilling degree of awareness will be motivated to contribute to the welfare of their community and the family of humanity. The attributes of the individuated person are present in a healthy society. I would note that every analyst I know personally is vitally involved in the life of their community.

Another criticism is that so much self-preoccupation takes up time and energy that could be spent on more altruistic goals. To that objection I would point out that people consume much time and energy in trying to distract themselves with misdirected preoccupations to relieve stress; they also expend energy seeking comfort or justification for psychosomatic, characterological, and neurotic problems. The energy would be well-spent in self-reflection. Insurance companies and physicians who encourage clients to seek psychotherapy and psychoanalysis save money and time spent on lost working hours, drugs, hospitalizations, and unproductive behavior.

When we closely examine the details of individuation, the inner/outer opposition disappears. For example, anger is a healthy instinct of self-preservation which can be expressed effectively or acted out unconsciously. "Should I express my anger in this situation or not? How should I do it and what will be the consequences?" By evaluating inner factors (the desire to express feelings) and outer factors (the inhibiting resistances), we unite the opposite forces by our reflection.

Movies illustrate the differences between generations in the blurring of inner and outer. "Billy Elliott" follows his inner promptings toward a career that his father found of no value. Eventually father comes to see the viability of the identity Billy has chosen. "The Waitress" learns to deliver herself from abusive relationships and develops her integrity. In "Darjeeling Limited" three brothers travel together and experience transforming changes in their self-images. They come to accept quite different values and identities of their places in the world and in the family than they could have ever admitted to before their journey. All of these characters effect a change in their families and environments. You can find examples of movies or novels that show how what was hidden becomes acceptable in a transformed worldview. It is easy to see the process of individuation working in great people—Buddha, Lincoln, Eleanor Roosevelt, Georgia O'Keeffe—but individuation is going on quietly in ordinary lives and communities.

II

Two Halves of Life

When reminded that Aristotle said a drama should have three parts, a beginning, a middle, and an end, the film director Jean-Luc Godard responded, "But not necessarily in that order." (Als, "Intruder in the Wings," p. 82.)

Jung thought that life had a natural beginning, middle, and end. We may, like Godard, want to question that order. Jung saw that in the first half of life—about 35 years—the psychic energy automatically and naturally directs itself toward making and maintaining a survival-oriented ego structure. That would involve forming a consistent identity; learning to distinguish reality from fantasy; becoming relatively self-sufficient; coping with the ups and downs of relationships and fate; negotiating one's bodily needs; expressing desires and getting satisfaction; figuring out the optimal degree of disclosure one could allow through one's social mask (persona); and the optimal amount of reward one could achieve through competence and accomplishments. With the ego well-established, we could expect to have found a good adjustment in the world.

Some ways that people have told me that they picture that ego-complex within themselves are: the computer system that sorts out communications; the mediator that negotiates with the inner world of instincts and the outer world of persona; the platoon leader who manages a group of rambunctious sub-personalities; the CEO who keeps order in the many departments of the mind—including public relations (the persona) and the business ledger (reality principle); the reasonable and loving parent of a large family.

Ego development was pictured in Jung's schema originally as a hero's adventure in battling the regressive forces of the unconscious—that aggressive hero who opposes the lazy-hazy drifting that drags us into complacency, passivity, dependence, addiction, and stagnation, or unbridled passions, or, as one client put it, "that dragon that sits on top of me." To meet those regressive suctions with active determination and will that surges as a life force in the form of psychic energy was seen as the goal of the first half of life.

There are problems with this model. One is that the "heroic attitude" demeans the "lazy-hazy" attitude, which may be the necessary context for a fertile creative process going on at a deeper level of awareness. Young people who are quiet and passive may be internally busy, not deficient. Another problem is that it became too easy to attach the ego to a stereotypical masculine image and the unconscious to a stereotypical feminine, seeing, for example, the male ego battling its feminine temptations or the dragon as a devouring mother to be slain. So much wariness of the regressive forces of the unconscious can foster an overly rational attitude of independence and detached objectivism that diminishes the value of connection to others. We might get the impression that attachment to loved ones, the family, and the community is immature.

According to Jung, midlife brings up doubts, questions, and uneasiness, because, Jung thought, the energy was beginning naturally to turn inward, away from the comfortable adjustments one had had to make in order to meet outer expectations. One became interested in exploring the underside of the consistent identity, the unlived dreams, the roads not traveled, the functions not explored—"the midlife crisis." This reversal of energies Jung saw as the work of the Self in its attempt to round out the personality, to seek a more complete personality which was not concerned only with achievement, survival, and appearances, but with a desire to open oneself to soul searching and exploring a relationship with the larger consciousness. Beginning at midlife, the larger picture, the Self, or the image of union and completion, holds the center of attention, instead of the constricted and self-serving ego.

This neat schema does not fit so neatly in 21st century society. There is in the 21st century a broader definition of acceptable behavior, greater understanding of personality types, and more tolerance for people who are unconventional than there was in the 20th. If your creative work or ambitions do not fit in with achieving security by your mid-thirties, it is not necessarily a failure of first-half-of-life tasks.

In Jung's day most young adults were expected to find a lifelong career and a mate. That cannot be taken for granted today. Now a combination of overpopulation, a competitive milieu, and fast-paced change in all areas of life make those achievements unattainable for many.

Many capable young adults do not find a career or a mate, and many do not see a permanent career or mate as a desirable thing. They prefer to enjoy multiple relationships and jobs, and modern life allows them the freedom to do so.

Fifty years ago I thought that if I studied for a doctoral degree I would probably quash any chance I had for marriage. I believed, as many people did, that no man would marry a bookish and ambitious woman. Besides, I would be in my mid-twenties when I finished my degree, and that would almost be too late to marry. I did very much want marriage and family but took a chance on following my inclination to study psychology just the same. I was lucky and relieved to find that my belief was wrong and that to some men, an intellectual woman was appealing. Now, mid-twenties is considered young to marry.

Previous eras saw unmarried people and childless couples as exceptions to the rule, and often in the case of single people, as somewhat inferior and dependent on others. The extended lifespan of today and the choices of contraception available create positive and negative effects: young adults have great freedom of choice and the opportunity to reinvent themselves repeatedly; on the downside, the luxury of making a decision of any kind as a young adult which one can count on to hold for the next fifty years is rare indeed.

The idea of reaching a level of stability and security which will allow us to sit back at middle age and meditate on the unlived life has become, for most of us, a farfetched fantasy. Jobs, marriages, relationships, and investments rarely remain secure today, and people struggle for a lifetime with the tasks that Jung considered first-half-of-life tasks.

Still, research shows that bilateralization of the brain occurs more between the ages of forty and sixty. Good brain functioning is increased as the frontal cortex becomes actively engaged in decision making, debating ideas, staying involved in solving conflicts, and being exposed to thoughtful issues and values, supporting Jung's notion.

There are vast class differences as the gap between the "haves" and the "have-nots" widens. The need and possibility for independence varies. In affluent groups, independence is delayed while education is the goal. Many people are well into adulthood before standing on their own while they debate their choices of occupation, whereas deprived youngsters have independence forced upon them before reaching adolescence with little or no freedom to choose a career. The extended lifespan has created many families who rely on their youth to care for their aged, or the aged to care for their grandchildren because life has become impossible for their parents.

In all classes there are so many opportunities and models for personality identity that young people may take on a number of personas and have trouble settling on one consistent personality structure. Advertising by image-makers is so strong that we are tempted to continue changing who we think we are long into adulthood. Middle-aged people can change careers, marital partners, sexual identities, faces, and bodily forms without a great deal of reflection. Tattoos and body art reflect the spiritual hunger to create, even unconsciously, a feeling of stability and a permanent mark of identity.

We are exposed to so much information that it is not unusual for children to be attracted to the spiritual questing that marks Jung's second-half-of-life tasks and to postpone the practical reality of making an independent living till late in life. This is particularly true when no easy career choice is available. On the other hand, many of us are so preoccupied with the dazzling opportunities for ego-aggrandizement that persist in dangling themselves before us that we never get around to the tasks of the second half. In fact, pop-culture encourages us to deny being in the second half of life altogether by presenting opportunities for prolonging youthful activities and appearances, having cosmetic surgery, and faking our age whenever possible.

Jacobi describes the task of the second half of life as raising the God-images to consciousness and establishing a constant contact between ego and Self, giving the ego an inner certainty and feeling of security as though contained in an all-embracing whole. But there are so many skeptical voices, voices declaring that God-images are of no value to our existence, and, in fact, that religion has brought on many wars, that many people shy away from religion altogether and never attempt to attain contact with a transcendent Self in the form of a religion or God. They not only do not value the experience of awe in the idea of a holy union with a transcendent other, they actually draw away from such experiences, believing them to be abnormal. They may put in its place a devotion to some concrete type of power, such as identifying with a celebrity, a political party, an athletic team, or some aspect of ego that takes on inflated proportions like becoming a leader in one's field or attaining a great amount of wealth. While such ambitions are not to be criticized, they do not reflect the individuation process as Jung meant it, because they sustain effort on the level of ego-development rather than through contact with a larger consciousness.

A young woman became upset because she had had this experience: while walking across her college campus one sunny day, she suddenly felt she was part of some large constellation of connection with everyone and everything around her. What could have been relished as a momentary glimpse of the eternal soul, this poor coed took as a sign that she was going crazy. Steeped in materialism with no knowledge of common mystical or poetic states, she took such an uninvited change of consciousness, which was not drug-induced, as pathology.

Does all this disprove Jung's notion of the movement of psychic energy during the two halves of life? Not necessarily, but we need to be less rigid in thinking about the progression/regression pattern and see that in our current society it does not necessarily happen once at midlife, but perhaps over and over in a person's life. Modern times call for a much more flexible attitude toward identity. The ego of the 1900s does not suit the 2000s. Today's egos must be like our luggage—light, resilient, stress resistant, ready to be clobbered over and over, and tolerant of ambiguity.

The fact that this is hard to manage for many who have had less than ideal circumstances for secure ego development may be why anxiety and depression are pandemic. Perhaps the need for inner support leads us to seek God-images much earlier in life. It is also possible that the ego relinquishes sovereignty to the Self to the detriment of its own development in the world of human commerce, and so remains ineffective as an individual personality, as in the case of sacrificing personal health and safety to be in the presence of a celebrity or attached to some important figure, gang, fundamentalist religion, or cult.

The sacrifice of ego called for in individuation requires the establishment of a healthy ego to begin with, so that sacrifices are not impulsive or self-destructive, but carefully weighed in with the desired effect on the larger society. With as much freedom to change as affluent societies have today, can a consistent Self as the ground of psychic security exist? How can there be a principle of order informing our lives if we are constantly changing? The answer may be that, as we experience ourselves changed, but also as the same consistently present person, a unifying principle can theoretically encompass all the changes.

The failure of consistent personality is another question. The inability to function with integrity as a result of brain disorders and psychoses does challenge the notion of a principle of order in the psyche. On the other hand, it reinforces the fact that a principle of order exists in union between mind and body and is conspicuous in its absence. A healthy brain displays the existence of a Self, as does an integrated personality, no matter how many changes and reinventions take place in that person's life. The exceptions due to illness must be seen as unfortunate aspects of the dark mysteries of death and disease which humankind has not been, and may never be, able to transcend. Another approach to devastation of identity through illness is to imagine a detached Nature at work in her varieties of experimental possibilities, always evolving exceptions and new forms.

Some atheists tell me that they disagree with Jung's notion that we have an innate, instinctual need for a spiritual attitude. They do not identify such a need in themselves, so they do not regard the spiritual instinct as universal, and therefore prefer to put their energy into being as comfortable as possible in the physical world of creature comforts. They do not see the purpose of connecting with a Self. Perhaps they project the Self onto some egoic purpose, an aesthetic or value system. Or perhaps they repress the instinct for a spiritual attitude. Or perhaps Jung was wrong in thinking the spiritual instinct was present in every human being.

Although Jung tried to allow for flexibility in his concept of individuation, one can get the impression that there is a fixed order to the unfolding of the unconscious in the process of individuation, especially as it is followed in analysis. Often it is presented as if one goes through clear stages and first discovers the Persona, then the Shadow, then the Anima and Animus, then the Self. Few processes can be described so explicitly by analysts today, and other non-linear models are favored, leaving room for individual differences.

> *Come gather 'round people*
> *Wherever you roam*
> *And admit that the waters*
> *Around you have grown*
> *And accept it that soon*
> *You'll be drenched to the bone.*
> *If your time to you*

Is worth savin'
Then you better start swimmin'
Or you'll sink like a stone
For the times they are a-changin'.

–Bob Dylan

12

Sexual Identity

Annus Mirabilis

Sexual intercourse began
In nineteen sixty-three
(Which was rather late for me) –
Between the end of the Chatterley ban
And the Beatles' first L.P.

Up till then there'd only been
A sort of bargaining,
A wrangle for a ring ,
A shame that started at sixteen
And spread to everything.

Then all at once the quarrel sank:
Everyone felt the same,
And every life became
A brilliant breaking of the bank,
A quite unlosable game.

So life was never better than
In nineteen sixty-three
(Though just too late for me)—
Between the end of the Chatterley ban
And the Beatles' first L.P.

–Philip Larkin
"Annus Mirabilis"
in *Collected Poems*

An important aspect of Jung's worldview is the gender archetype; he called it the "syzygy," from the Greek, meaning "a pair of opposites." The gender archetype consists of masculine and feminine principles which manifest physically through sexual characteristics and also through psychological characteristics. Throughout most of the plant and animal kingdom the contrasts between masculine and feminine are usually clear, and in previous times, so was the case in humans, at least superficially. Women and men appeared different in body and dress and displayed different interests and aptitudes, and Jung's expectation was that an important part of becoming as conscious as possible was coming to know the opposite sex as it was present within one's personality. For most people this took a deliberate effort to become conscious of less obvious or even hidden characteristics of the opposite sex within oneself.

In the early twentieth century heterosexuality was the mark of psychological maturity. Freud's goal of psychosexual development was the stage of "genitality"; it meant being comfortably fulfilled in a heterosexual relationship. Jung did not agree with such a narrow criterion, but he was limited to a conventional view of sexuality as one would expect of a respected member of a conventional Swiss community. Conformity did not go so far as to prevent him from having a mistress, but it did not open him to endorse homosexuality as a normal way of life. Yet, Jung made progress toward awareness of the bisexual nature of human beings by recognizing the Dionysian component in the psyche (more about this in Part III, Chapter 4). Jung particularly tried to bring the feminine principle into equal status with the masculine.

It is not stated directly in any considerations of the classical individuation process, but it is now unthinkable to omit a discussion of sexual preferences in examining the fullness of personality development. Being unwed, divorced, promiscuous, asexual, homosexual, or bisexual could have been grounds for a diagnostic label in 1900. Today we consider the psyche intricate enough to contain numerous sexual arrangements and possibilities within the normal range. Each of us has our reasons for our preferences, and some, according to neurological research, have had those reasons established before birth.

Although the way of individuation can be more chaotic and bewildering currently, we fortunately have the freedom to find our way sexually without apology. Probably for many people born before 1960 the notion of transgendering is bizarre. In mid-twentieth century schools of education, teachers were taught that sexual identity was not firmly established in children until age three, when they became aware of genital differences, and then it was expected to be stable for life. Of course, little boys would see that they were built differently from girls, and that made them male, and little girls would do the same. The popular children's television personality, Mr. Rogers, sang, "Boys are fancy on the outside. Girls are fancy on the inside. Everybody's fancy. Everybody's fine. Your body's fancy and so is mine!"

The struggle for acceptance of homosexuality has been a hard-won battle, insofar as it has been won. Until recently, no one inquired too closely about what we did in our bedrooms, but people suffered indignities and humiliation when their homosexuality was suspected. Now we are able to disclose and even celebrate our sexual preferences without provoking overt hostility. This is an enormous change in social mores.

On July 20, 2008, a news item on BBC reported that a man, who had been a woman but changed his identity while keeping his female reproduction system, gave birth to a healthy girl. This man is now married to a woman, and since we weren't told who the father of the child was, I assumed the father was not the nominal mother who had had a sex change without giving up his masculine reproductive system. The birth mother, from his masculine vantage point, reported that he will enjoy looking on while his daughter and her nominal mother bake cookies together. And so the stereotypes live on. The fact that we can now be obvious in our sexual preferences and even reconfigure ourselves to change not only our secondary sexual characteristics, but our genitalia, to meet some inner self-image, seems more than weird to those who have not experienced the tension of misplaced gender.

How can we understand the individuation process in this capacity to literally change sexual organs? This is a new phenomenon, and perhaps we need longer research periods to understand the impact on the life of a person having such a drastic physical transformation. Some say they regret having had transgender surgery; others report being more at peace after the gender change. We have to wonder whether much reflection and dialogue with the Self through dreams and inner work as well as relationship factors went on before the decision to change genders was made. We also have to wonder what happens in the conscious attitude in dealing with this tension through concretization of the solution as opposed to living with the tension and trying to resolve it on a psychological level. Androgynous singer-songwriter Antony Hegarty (and the Johnsons) looks at gender as a spiritual, not just physical, phenomenon. (Hegarty, "For Today I am a Boy.")

While Freudian theory is clear about what constitutes sexual perversions, Jung does not address the subject, but gives us reason to believe he accepts Freud's approach to seeing them as symptoms. In our permissive civilization we have difficulty drawing the line about where healthy diversity ends and pathology begins. Generally there is no argument about child sexual abuse, only about detecting it. The presence of religious cults within our democracy has raised thorny issues about how free such communities are to manipulate the lives of their children, such as marrying girls of thirteen to patriarchs. Those communities can point to the histories of kingdoms throughout the world that were propagated by children, such as the queen, married at fourteen to a French king, who bore seven children and died at age twenty-four.

Polygamy is against the law in some states, but is difficult to prosecute; law enforcement attacks the child abuse practices in such communities instead. At present the United States law protects children under age eighteen. Other countries have different age limits. The psyche's truth is not, of course, so cut and dried. Sexual maturity is an individual matter.

Forcing or seducing a child of any age into sexual activity is clearly a violation of the child's right to mature in a healthy way at his or her natural pace. For some it produces a lifetime of psychic and physical pain. However, I have seen some adults in psychotherapy who were able to overcome terrible sexual or physical abuse and neglect as children and to move on to a successful reflective individuation process, including good relationships with other adults.

For the perpetrators, however, the picture is troublesome and less clear. Channeling one's sexual energy into non-adult and inappropriate objects usually indicates a blocking of sexual and psychic energy which normally flows toward peers. Often the perpetrator has suffered childhood trauma which caused blocking and diverting of his or her sexual energy, and so the trauma is repeated for generations. The use of power in such acts between perpetrators and their subjects seems not just pathological but criminal by today's values. Yet such abuse of power has been approved throughout the ages as sex with children is ritualized or considered a right of adults in some cultures. This makes child pornography a thriving international business today.

Individuation implies integrity, ethical consideration, and concern about the welfare of others as well as oneself. Abusing children is not possible with such awareness. A young patient of mine recognized in himself the compulsion to have sex with children. He acknowledged his sexual blocks and immature development, but he had to worry about his behavior until such time as he could overcome his sexual problem, if ever. Psychoanalysis could not guarantee that he would. He had been a fine teacher, but in his struggle to keep himself away from temptation, he gave up his profession and entered into a contemplative religious community. That took integrity.

A history of abuse and violence that keeps trauma reverberating does not allow such awareness to develop, or if it does develop, to be sustained. If we look at the brain as a tripartite entity consisting of a lower brute survival section (the reptilian brain), a middle area mammalian section (the emotional brain), and a frontal reasoning section (the later-developing frontal cortex), we can understand how preoccupation with survival and conditioned fear keeps energy reverberating in the reptilian brain, to the detriment of higher functions, like caring about others and using reason and good judgment. Abuse begets abuse unless, through the effort of reflective individuation, we become aware of feelings like empathy and altruism, and we see the possibility that we can change our behavior.

Occasional deviant sexual behavior with another adult in a person who is capable of adult intimacy can be seen as a creative diversion. Psychoanalysis called this "regression in the service of the ego"; for example, sadomasochistic games, swinging, and other unconventional activities within the context of an intimate relationship or as occasional diversions are enjoyable to some. But if sexual deviancy is the *only* outlet for an individual's sexual energy, we have to wonder why someone avoids affection and intimacy with other adults that is the natural progression of human relatedness. We have to ask what could be interfering with that natural progression and keeping us preoccupied with early habits, perhaps out of fear, anger, and pure animal-level survival?

In contemporary life in most civilized countries we are free to enjoy a multiplicity of possible sexual expressions. However, in some societies today, people, especially women and children, have little or no freedom to develop sexually. Genital mutilation, clitorisectomies, sexual trafficking, and prostitution of young children are allowed, even promoted for money and the enjoyment of perverted adults. For the victims of these abuses, there is slim chance of ever enjoying a healthy sex life, and individuation can only proceed in an atmosphere of healing from trauma, suffering, and mourning that lost innocence to which the young are entitled. Our human species as a collective soul is responsible for caring with compassion for those traumatized, and for bringing, or at least offering, awareness to those perpetrators who have not experienced the capability to love and empathize with all beings.

> *The moon is always female and so*
> *am I although often in this vale*
> *of razorblades I have wished I could*
> *put on and take off my sex like a dress…..*
>
>   –Marge Piercy
>   from "The Moon is Always Female"

13

Relationship to the Collective

Do not take thought for your person or properties, but first chiefly
to care about the greatest improvement of your soul.

–Socrates

The days of the solitary individual, solitary tribe, or solitary nation are no more. There is no hidden private space. Yet we don't always feel a sense of belonging. Twentieth century Carl Jung worried about the individual being gobbled up by social role expectations, parental control, political movements, governments, or religious dogma. Having so many possibilities for projecting the Self onto another human body or institution threatens to drown out the voice of one's own soul. Today we appear to have many more opportunities to find our own way. In fact, we are bombarded with a plurality of social possibilities, a diversity of moral values to choose from, a bird's eye view of the earth and its peoples, and, rather than feeling too closely contained, we are more likely to feel too loosely connected, isolated and uncontained.

There are exceptions to such free space throughout the world: little children forced into military service or sexual trafficking, huge populations displaced and trapped in refugee camps for life, young people subscribing to the dictatorship of gangs as a substitute for family, the poor scraping out survival rations, those brainwashed by fundamentalist religions, the victims of totalitarian and greedy governors. In none of these situations do individuals have a choice over their own lives. Those of us fortunate enough to have had reflective individuation available to us have a responsibility to these, our human family who are still trapped in collective psychic prisons.

We also have the responsibility to understand the envy and hatred that our well-being provokes in the less fortunate, to meet their hatred with empathy and a commitment to non-violent work toward diplomatic transformation. To do such work without self-righteousness or a patronizing attitude is one task of our time. Other tasks are to identify our own unconscious imprisonment and to question the level of consciousness of our own communities.

In addition to helping to free those who are not allowed to have choices over their lives, we who are able need to look at the traps we ourselves are caught in, traps which sap our energies and seduce us into unconscious submission to projects we would not consciously support. Some of the traps are: consumerism; excessive use of medication and chemicals; cultural biases about what is "normal" and what is "pathological"; dependence on technology; addiction to instant communication; addiction to entertainment; addiction to noise.

Most of these traps come down to the insidious effects that advertising has over our values. For those of us old enough to remember a world in which we were not bombarded with advertising and constant input of information, it seems we, the human family, have lost a very valuable possession: the ability to appreciate quiet and solitude, once a condition that fostered pleasure in the creative process.

We also have witnessed the loss of ethical balance in the world of business, in spite of the concerns of John Waide ("The Making of Self and World in Advertising") and others like him. Not only does advertising invade our soul space; but like a Pied Piper, it leads our children into worlds that do not mirror our values.

A formidable barrier to individuation is consumerism. Jungian psychoanalyst Tom Kelly writes:

> Consuming, be it clothes, food, alcohol, or drugs, is the principal value and more often than not leads, like the uroborus eating its own tail, to the threat of being consumed by the dragon of debt....To what extent is it possible to genuinely become oneself when there is so much pressure to conform, to consume and to acquire? While people...are living longer, retiring earlier and having more leisure time, the primary concern seems to focus more on whether enough money has been saved than on spiritual development. (Kelly, lecture to Jung Society of Toronto.)

Kelly's concern is underlined by Jungian psychoanalyst Bernice Hill. She calls for the confrontation with consumerism by evoking a powerful inner value system to explore an enlightened relationship to money and acquisitions. In a small, powerful book, *Money and the Spiritual Warrior*, Hill has collected a number of resources that demonstrate an enlightened relationship to money and acquisitions. One source, the perspective of George Kinder, compares the evolution of the relationship to money with the chakra system. We begin with the need for survival and security and progress to the seventh chakra energies, which focus on the common good and the need to serve something greater than oneself.

Another resource is the way of Ted Mallon's *Journey Toward Masterful Philanthropy*, which demonstrates a relationship with money that might begin selfishly but culminates in an attitude of generosity, wisdom, and humility. Mallon's individuation process is an interesting journey in itself; it was jump-started by a number of traumas, one of which was being struck by lightning and having his energy transformed into a new system that is exquisitely receptive to a universal spiritual energy. His book illuminates his unique process of individuation.

Spiritual development presumes the capacity to relate to a spiritual Other or Others. In our current societies we are encouraged to identify *ourselves* as supreme beings, to focus all of our energies on aggrandizing the ego as *ourselves*. After all, we humans have conquered nature and gained dominion over all other forms of life (except vermin, viruses, bacteria, cancer cells, etc., but they don't count!). Surely we are worthy of recreating an environment to meet our needs for immediate comfort and gratification, regardless of the cost to nature and the future generations, aren't we? Well, no, as a matter of fact; awareness of the legacy we leave to future generations is an aspect of personality completion. If we have become identified with the Self (as opposed to being in relationship to the Self) and so deny the need to consider others, we have succumbed to superhuman arrogance. We might spend a lifetime devoted to making a god of the perfect body, the greatest amount of wealth, or the most beautiful estate, but we will not likely find ultimate gratification there.

Polly Young-Eisendrath explains that biological determinism has done great harm by promoting a belief that suffering can only be relieved by biological intervention, and not by a change in awareness or attitude. She writes:

> If you explain suffering only in organic terms, then you exclude the possibility that you can change your life through changing your mind. If you further believe that the world's goods are worth acquiring, you will eventually

> face the fact that individual and collective resources are
> depleted...a unique problem of our period of time: human
> suffering without interest in its origins or knowledge about
> its causes. (Young-Eisendrath and Muramoto, eds., *Awaken-
> ing and Insight: Zen Buddhism and Psychotherapy*, p. 71.)

Growth and progress once seemed inherently positive, associated
with life and hope. But we have seen growth become monstrous. More
can be less. Land developers and ego-psychologists seem equally unaware of the dangers of over-growth. As James Hillman writes in *Kinds
of Power*, "Victorious conquests and the grandiosity of expansionism no
longer carry the national honor." (Hillman, *Kinds of Power*, p. 48.)

Neither do the masters of denial who display what Hillman calls
"psychological capitalism," cutting quality of life and soul to increase
some notion of productivity. Included in this is the medical community to the extent it has been co-opted by pharmaceutical companies
and refuses patients the time and energy it takes to hear their stories
and help them find alternative means to problem-solving. Many ail-
ments brought on by stress and unhealthy living could be cured without medicines with a holistic approach which encourages looking at
reasons for symptoms, such as anxiety, and learning to handle them
through inner processing.

The educational and medical professions also display a bias in valuing extroverted action above introverted contemplation, instead of
valuing them as different ways of psychological processing which are
equally valid. The mental health professionals responsible for the *Diagnostic and Statistical Manual* (DSM) for classifying mental illnesses considered describing introversion as a symptom of disorder, rather than
an adaptive personality trait which has great value in some situations
and in some cultures. Our schools reward outgoing students who adapt
quickly to prescribed methods and disfavor those with individualistic, sometimes more thoughtful, learning styles. We even go so far as
to medicate those pupils who respond differently or unexpectedly to
classroom procedures — at what cost to creativity?

Another possible barrier to individuation is technology. In itself
neutral, technology can be used to avoid or enhance opening the soul's
vista. As an expression of human creativity, technology is the brilliant
result of the soul's fascination with matter and the impulse to keep
refining pleasure. But there is a point at which the price of technology

will be too high for the soul's home on this planet to support. We may have already reached that point. But as we continue to survive and at least assume that we have still some choice about this, how should we act?

I would say there is one major key to aiming our world on a trajectory of survival instead of destruction: to view the human race as our "tribe" deserving of loyalty with an attitude of cooperation rather than competition. This has not been the American way. Our country has thrived and led the world with its lively competitive spirit. Not doing away with that spirit, but carefully choosing where to use it, choosing to be generous rather than powerful, would be a move toward survival. Sometimes there is more strength in being humble than in being right and power-filled. We could first be aware of our thoughtless expenditures on energy sources and technology that benefit only the profit motive and not the welfare of the community and the human family. We could put pressure on government and corporations in every conceivable way, including civil activism, voting, and choosing what we support financially, to change policies and to encourage wholesome forms of technology.

On an individual basis we could realize that we do not have to live as the majority live, but can be mindful of our uses of technology in very simple ways. Choosing to think about what we are doing instead of following the crowd is the mark of individuation. Doing things by hand and slowly is usually more fulfilling in the long run, but requires a change in attitude from having to accomplish too much in a given time in order to compete. That is a hard trap to escape when we are being constantly told that we can do it all and have it all. And have it immediately! Such claims are a destructive seduction.

The Calming Thought of All

That coursing on, whate'er men's speculations,
Amid the changing schools, theologies, philosophies,
Amid the bawling presentations new and old
The round earth's silent vital laws, facts, modes continue.

                                                            –Walt Whitman

14

World Cultures

Interviewed on his 90th birthday, Nelson Mandela, the South African political leader who led the fight against apartheid, was asked if he regretted not having spent more time with his family during his lifetime. He thought for a while and replied, "No, I had to do what was necessary for my soul." (Interview, British Broadcasting Corporation, June, 2008.)

Jung was clear about the fact that he was proposing individuation from the standpoint of a Western European cultural lens, and he did not mean to apply it to other cultures. And even as the world has become smaller, we Jungians recognize that our precise notions about individuation cannot be applied to all cultures without significant reworking. Yet it is possible that, since the concept applies to human consciousness, it might be adapted to describe the expansion of consciousness in whatever form is available in any given culture. This is an aspect of the concept that needs more research.

In the Western European and American tradition, a commonly desired characteristic of individuation is the capability of persons to leave their parental home and make their way as independent individuals in a home separate from the family of origin. Naturally, geographical distance from the family is not what Jung meant by individuation. We may put miles between us and still stay emotionally dependent on each other. But being true to our values often means changing our profession, religion, politics, or attitudes to something entirely different from what was expected of us in our family.

In some cultures that kind of independence is discouraged, because one's first duty is to help preserve the welfare of the family of origin, to stay with the family, clan, or tribe and contribute to the well-being of the group. Survival demands it. This describes the Pakistani woman mentioned in a previous section who could not oppose her tribal requirement of arranged marriage. (This is so common in Britain that they have enacted a "Forced Marriage Act" to protect women.) Loyalty is also highly valued in cultures that have experienced genocide, as have Native-Americans, Jews, Kurds, and minority groups in many countries.

In spite of family prohibitions, some individuals are capable of seeing beyond their environmental restrictions, even when they do not choose to openly oppose them. Some can and do make contact with a wider consciousness and use their dreams, creative abilities, and ambitions to compromise with the conscious situation. They may become prominent as spokespersons, leaders, or advocates for others, or they may express their advanced consciousness as introversion through art, healing, and ways of wisdom. As long as the possibility of thinking for oneself is available, individuation can proceed, as Mandela's statement illustrates. But it may look different in different cultures, including some parts of the USA and Western Europe.

Actually, contemporary trends in psychoanalysis have moved more and more toward encouraging community, a generous and open-spirited attitude toward others and toward nature, and a support for flexibility-oriented, rather than goal-oriented, individuation. These values are easier to express in parts of the world that haven't been entrenched in authoritarian values.

In general, Native-Americans' process of individuation appears different from that of European-Americans. Because of their experience of the near extinction of their culture, many Native-Americans expect to adhere closely to the traditions of their nations. They value the continuation of those values and rituals which connect them to their heritage, although they may feel encouraged to leave their culture to experience and learn the ways of the larger society. Often Native-Americans become active politically in order to promote the good of their people and contribute to the development of their nations. This is not to imply that they do not also identify themselves as Americans, as illustrated by their participation in military combat and national politics.

An intellectual dilemma brought about through the mind-body split, begun with Plato and thoroughly developed by Descartes, had an impact on Western minds through the Enlightenment. This split with the world of nature was not suffered by non-Europeans such as Native American, African, and Asian cultures, and the differences are apparent in attitudes toward matter and nature to this day.

Jungian psychoanalyst Jerome Bernstein, who has worked for years with the Navajo Native-Americans, believes that the Western ego takes its form and dynamic structure at the price of its separation from nature. Thus, individuation as Jung formulated it has a lot to do with reconnecting to that dimension of the transpersonal, the objective psyche, or Self as nature.

Says Bernstein:

> As I see it, much of what the individuation process aims at is the starting point for the (traditionally rooted) Navajo. Much of the connection that the Western individuation process aims at is where they begin—albeit with a different ego structure than the Western ego. There is no separation from nature, no differentiation between mind and body, between the ego and the sacred. (Bernstein, private communication.)

It seems safe to say that an individual can proceed with a strong sense of community and loyalty to the collective without losing one's individuality. Bernstein has written extensively about the split between humans and nature that is so prevalent in our society and the difficulty encountered by people who are sensitive to that split in his book, *Living in the Borderland: The Evolution of Human Consciousness and the Challenge of Healing Trauma.*

In the United States we are expected to ignore a heavy-handed approach to environmental problems, an approach that assumes an attitude of domination and greed instead of conservation and care. Those who feel empathy with nature and distress about the destruction are often dismissed as abnormally sensitive, and they are misunderstood and marginalized. Actually, like canaries in the mine, many are more realistic about consequences than those in denial of the destruction, and they have important information if we could only listen.

Values that were assumed by our culture to be universal fifty years ago now seem terribly biased. Colonialism viewed culture through the eyes of the colonists and distorted the nature of the colonized, at great cost to the colonized and to humanity itself. European and American countries applied their values to African and Asian cultures with little consideration of history. Corporations saw the value of their commercial goods through their vision, which did not benefit their customers or the environment. Men made laws which did not consider the welfare of women, and women promoted customs which did not fit the needs of men. We are all being shown the possibility of seeing through the eyes of others, seeing from another angle, seeing from a larger vantage point.

We cannot undo the damage, cannot restore the broken communities and ecosystems, cannot revive the victims of genocide who have had their ways of life annihilated. What we can do is stop imposing and judging, and start to wait, listen, and respect the habits and philosophies of people with different values.

Jung emphasized "uniting the opposites" in becoming a whole person. He meant that we come to see nuances, rather than engaging in black and white thinking. We are less rigid about what is good or bad, or what constitutes masculine or feminine traits, less occupied with separating human and nature. In Native-American pre-colonial philosophy there has been no separation to be overcome between ego and nature, between human life and animal life, between the welfare of the person and the welfare of humankind. Until recent years our government has systematically silenced and tried to eradicate the Native-Americans' capacity to articulate their philosophy. Now some leaders see that there was wisdom in the attitudes of native peoples toward nature that we would not allow, but which was valuable. This has happened in other parts of the world as well, such as Australia. There the prime minister recently made a sincere and very moving public apology to the indigenous people for the way they had been treated by their colonizing government. Many of the political problems in the Middle East are a result of misunderstanding the values of people whose allegiance has been to their tribal identities for generations.

C. Michael Smith writes that tribal myths and rituals through the life stages provide support for the transformation of individuals in tribal communities. He points out that, although tribal societies stress participation in the collective, there is considerable value placed upon inner experience:

> ... in native North American tribes there has been an emphasis on personal interior experience through vision quests. Meaningful contact with nominal entities such as ancestral spirits, power animals, and the like, are encouraged, and this personal religious experience is highly valued because it is believed to serve the individual and social

good.... It would appear that the main difference between
the personal development process of traditional (tribal) societies and that required by the individuation process is
a matter of accent. In tribal societies the accent appears
to be on the collective participation. In the Jungian view
of individuation, the accent is on the differentiation from
the collective. (Smith, *Jung and Shamanism in Dialogue*, p.
119-120.)

Professor of psychology Roger Brooke lived in Africa as a child. He
notes that Jung's approach to individuals and community reveals a suspicious bias toward the collective as exerting a regressive pull on the
individual; Brooke sees Jung's bias as a "colonialism of the psyche."
Like many early explorers and social scientists, Jung thought of native
peoples as "primitive" and inferior in ego-development. We now know
that this bias resulted from not being able to see beyond one's own
cultural norms. Although Jung admired the ability of native people to
maintain their connection with nature, with the spiritual instinct, and
with their ancestry, from today's perspective it seems Jung devalued the
role of a community in facilitating the individuation process.

In contrast to the colonialists' view of the inferiority of indigenous
people, Brooke describes his illiterate African housekeeper: her memory
was prodigious, her understanding of political realities was sophisticated, her ethical thinking was finely differentiated; in effect, her ego
functioned as well as or better than many educated people, and her
individuality was well developed, while she followed the traditional
customs with devotion.

Brooke maintains that, despite its bias, Jung's psychology has the
potential to support an individuation that promotes bringing the world
into oneself in a larger consciousness, one that finds communion with
the larger world. He introduces the Zulu term *Ubuntu*, which translates
as sense of community, of responsibility toward others and toward the
wider world, and toward a sense of self-realization. Brooke says:

African humanism, evoked by the term Ubuntu, would
imagine individuation as a process of personal growth and
transformation within the network of relationships that
make such transformation possible and to which the person remains, therefore, ethically indebted... if we imagine
individuation through the notion of Ubuntu, then there
is no heroic loneliness, no growing separation from others

regarded as a "herd." Individuated consciousness is certainly not the dispassionate rationality of science. In Ubuntu consciousness, all the virtues we admire are present: personal responsibility, ethical self-knowledge, strength and courage, humility, forgiveness, human understanding, a knowledge of history, and a sense of the sacred. (Brooke, *Pathways to Integrity*, pp. 49-50.)

In collaboration with African healers, Jungian analyst Peter Ammann arranged for some of them to describe their process of becoming healers. (Conference workshop, The International Association for Jungian Studies / International Association for Analytical Psychology conference, Zurich, Switzerland, July, 2008.) The Africans explained that they were chosen by the ancestors, who called them to divination and the capacity to diagnose illness. They told us that they believe that God created communities, not individuals, as no one can exist alone. Therefore when the ancestors call—which they may do at any time— one should answer for the good of the community. However, some do resist the call, for the road of healer is a hard road; perhaps this might be compared with refusing the individuation process. The ancestors call in different ways, often through a great dream, or by causing the chosen one to become dizzy and fall asleep, and being given the message in the sleeping or trance state.

The ancestral world is very much a reality in the psyche of tribal peoples, and having children to perpetuate the society is paramount in importance. Death for them is a transition into the world of the ancestors, where they remain part of their community. Peter Ammann reminded us that Jung spoke of the unconscious as the link to the ancestors, and of our souls and bodies being composed of individual elements combined with age-old components from the ancestors. Jung said that the two-million-year-old man speaks through us in dreams. In listening to the healers describe their work, it was obvious that they maintain a dialogue with the Self as they experience it. They appear to possess great ego strength and seemed competent and capable of individuation by our Western world standards.

Grinnell notes that the animal soul of man descends through the ages and includes all life: the single cells, the crustaceans, cold-blooded, mammalian, and hominoid creatures. (Grinnell, *Alchemy in a Modern Woman*, pp. 88-94). When we allow ourselves to alter consciousness as shamans do, we are able to access these deeper levels and sense the experience of our other souls, animal or human. This is why certain seers and psychics are able to hear, see, or feel their way into the experience of another person or animal.

Consciousness that is deliberately curtailed by grave prohibitive measures, such as brain-washing and systematic thought control, makes individuation impossible. People who are subjected to fanatical ideologies are in danger of not being able to have the intellectual tools to individuate. An essential aspect of good ego functioning is the ability to think logically.

A study of people in fanatical societies by Lawrence Alschuler showed that fanaticism could be described as "repressed doubt"; in other words, the subjects of fanaticism were afraid to allow themselves to doubt; they had to forbid themselves from using that valuable thought process of thinking logically so as not to disturb the system of thought they were taught. (Alschuler, "Jung and Politics," Lecture given at The International Association for Jungian Studies / International Association for Analytical Psychology conference, Zurich, Switzerland, July, 2008.) Only those who had enough ego strength to assert themselves in the face of conflict and humiliation brought on by expressing doubt experienced any feeling of freedom. Those who were completely rooted in ancestral heritage and had no ego strength to face oppression by dominant members could be said to have used the ancestral connection as a Self, whereas those with stronger egos could experience the ancestral roots as flexible and supportive in the face of conflict and be healed of their fanatical ideas.

People who have lived in democratic countries for generations, if they have not been subjected to repressive ideologies, have a hard time getting their minds around the habits of thinking that are evoked by a totalitarian government. The suspiciousness, fear of self-exposure, and even paranoia encouraged by living in a totalitarian milieu are impossible for most free people to identify with. In authoritarian cultures, cunning self-promotion is the rule, not individuation as we know it with its capacity for empathy and intimacy, which are seen as weaknesses by power-mongers. Suspiciousness becomes habitual and is slow to change, even when restrictions are lifted. Generations may have their thought processes impaired.

In some totalitarian regimes, for example, children were encouraged to report their own parents for anything considered subversive. The very foundations of personal integrity, that is, close interpersonal ties, were undermined, as children were claimed by devotion to the abstract ideology of the government at the expense of affection and loyalty. A basic freedom necessary for individuation is the right to privacy, and this does not exist in authoritarian cultures. The Self is assumed by the State.

Yet we in our sophisticated democracies are not immune to brainwashing. (See Chapter 13, "Relationship to the Collective.")

> There is a causal linkage between individuation, conscientization, and democracy. I believe that this causal linkage invites further research and promises to make Jungian psychology even more relevant to the study of politics. (Lawrence Alschuler in *The Cambridge Companion to Jung*, Young-Eisendrath and Dawson, eds., p. 292.)

Janet Dallett relates how the dominant parent of psychotic children unconsciously communicates three things to them:

> 1) the parent has superior knowledge, ability, and expertise in all matters, and it must never be challenged; 2) dire consequences will ensue if the child engages in independent or creative activity not sanctioned by the parent, and, 3) the child is weak, defective, or otherwise inferior, but is nonetheless deeply loved by the all-powerful parent. (Dallett, private communication.)

If we apply these attitudes to group leaders, it becomes apparent that leaders who are non-disclosing, who discourage questions and disagreements, who encourage fear in the populace, who play on the idea that those who are different or unconventional are threats to the general public, and who present themselves as powerful protectors, in turn create citizens who begin to react like psychotic children, projecting the image of infallible parents on their leaders and avoiding thinking creatively. The psychologist Murray Stein has written:

> Individuation is not optional, not conditioned, not subject to vagaries of cultural differences. It is essential. (Stein, *Journal of Jungian Theory and Practice*, p. 3.)

To summarize the essence of this chapter, our view of individuation includes the awareness that self-realization is a right of every human being and is a fragile thing. Vigilance is required to protect it. Individuation is not about being grand. It requires that we become aware of how unconscious we are, how we may give up control of our minds and lives without questioning it unless we keep trying to be conscious. Individuation allows us to expand our vision and our circle of concern.

> The flower of tolerance to see and appreciate cultural diversity is one flower we can cultivate for the children of the twenty-first century. Another flower is the truth of suffering—there has been so much unnecessary suffering in our century. If we are willing to work together and learn together, we can all benefit from the mistakes of our time, and, seeing with the eyes of compassion and understanding, we can offer the next century a beautiful garden and a clear path. (Thich Nhat Hanh, *Peace is Every Step*, p. 134.)

15

Individuation: Heroic and Mercurial

"Growth" suggests a linear process. This is natural to the biological model. We say to the youngster we haven't seen in a few years, "How tall you've become!" That is the obvious, but so many other essential aspects of the youth have changed. As adults our outer changes are slow, but our inner growth can zoom ahead without any noticeable traces to the observer. We can remember attitudes we held or decisions we made just a few years before that we believed to be very mature, but that seem immature to us now. In the example of expanding awareness, the up/down style of measurement does not seem appropriate. Truer spatial images would be of a widening circle, or a spiral movement around a center.

While Freud thought it was all downhill after we reached the peak of psychological growth, adult genitality, Jung saw that we can grow in psychic awareness till consciousness is—or appears to be—snuffed out completely. I said "appears to be" because the state of consciousness in others is unfathomable. However, information from brain studies is rapidly increasing, and confirms that good brain functioning increases well into old age when we keep the frontal cortex actively engaged – such as through decision making, debating ideas, confronting problems, staying involved in thoughtful issues and values, i.e., in reflective individuation.

When we are around people with dementia we may see psychological changes and emotional or spiritual development continuing despite the disease that interferes with memory and reasoning; sometimes something is still being observed and registered. Brain imaging now shows that a person in a coma may register changes in the brain's motor cortex when stimulated with pictures of movement. We have no way of knowing if anything is registering consciously or if anything progressive or constructive is happening in the person's being.

Jill Taylor, a physician, described her state of consciousness while suffering a stroke. (Taylor, *My Stroke of Insight.*) Although she could not communicate, her right brain was recording and responding to her condition in an unusually responsive way. Her logical processes were not functioning well, but her emotional brain was intact and extremely sensitive. She was not able to convey her experience until she recovered, but then she eloquently articulated the transformation she underwent in her ability to appreciate the unity of being.

Developmental psychology focuses on the linear type of growth process of the psyche. It is intrinsically linked with time and aging, even if not directly in a one–to-one fashion. Abraham Maslow noted that, when we have fundamental needs met at one level of conscious development, we are able to move to another level, a "hierarchy of needs." All such systems show development from less to more. Each stage includes the one before.

To understand why I am using the term "mercurial individuation," let us review the historical development of the concept of individuation. We observed a long history of interest in the invisible or psychic reality from the time of the earliest Greek philosophers and Asian philosophies, and through the ideas of medieval scholars, and the Hebrew, Christian, and Islamic mystics. The early science of alchemy continued to combine psychological with physical imagery.

With the Enlightenment, science grew more sophisticated and impressive, and, strengthened by opposition from the Church, split from the inclusion of psychic reality to deal only with tangible facts. The philosophy of logical positivism dominated cultural thought with its values of determinism and certainty. Some philosophers have challenged the idea of an individual identity altogether; they see "identity" as inseparable from an interdependent and relational world. The individual is in constant interplay with experience and is merely an interpreter, not a synthesizer of internal events.

At the same time social movements were changing the focus of society from the authoritarian state to the individual citizen. There was a backlash to the positivism of the Enlightenment from the Romanticists. In America the Transcendentalist movement echoed the values of Romanticism.

Freud and Jung introduced the idea that unconscious elements influence the thoughts that we *think* are logical. Regardless of what Freud and Jung observed in their patients, they were obliged to present their ideas in positivistic terms in order to be respected by scientists. But the notion of unconscious influence put all rational systems on shaky ground. Freud, with his background in biology, maintained the rational, scientific attitude. Jung presented himself as an empirical scientist, but, with his background in religious and psychic experiences, could not refrain from championing the reality of the psyche and introducing a spiritual factor. Nevertheless, there was a bias among the early followers of Jung to color the concepts with the fixity and certainty typical of that era and also to reflect authoritarian and patriarchal attitudes of the time. This led to criticism from feminists as well as from proponents of a more flexible, less calcified approach to the psyche.

The new physics of relativity meant the collapse of the principles discovered by Newton, which had been thought to be immutable. The middle of the twentieth century saw the development of post-modernism, a reaction in intellectual communities to "certainty." Both Jungian and Freudian theorists began to consider the effects of chaos and relativity on the psyche. In the Jungian world the "archetypal approach" carried this trend, but the changes were minor compared to Freudian circles, where the shift in approach was dramatic. Never before had Freudian analysts dared to speak of religion and transcendence as acceptable subjects of study.

Freud's approach to religious experience was strictly positivistic. His most anti-religious text, *The Future of an Illusion*, brought him into conflict with his friend, psychoanalyst Oskar Pfister, who argued that Freud's impression of religion was very limited. Another friend, Nobelist Romain Rolland, defended religion as an irreducible spiritual element in human experience, which is Jung's position. Rolland described "oceanic feeling" as the way spontaneous religion manifests. Other Freudians agreed that feelings of reverence and awe seek an outlet and argued that the transcendental experience is a legitimate subject of psychoanalysis. (See Part III, "Lagniappe," Chapter 17.)

In Jungian circles, the term "Archetypal Psychologies" is often used to describe Jungians who espouse diverse points of view rather than hewing to a single perspective; James Hillman is credited as the initiator of this approach. (Marlan, *Archetypal Psychologies*.) Archetypal Psychologies are an offspring of Einstein's era of relativity, which changed the way we think. We can no longer hold onto the notion of fixed space or constant time zones. Archetypal Psychologies are also the offspring of quantum theory, which describes the actions and relationships of unpredictable particles; like humans they act in patterns but maintain their individuality. Physicists and psychologists are in a similar position currently; both are operating without a permanent or fixed background.

Sometimes when we read the work of Jungians about individuation, we sense that there is a heroic bias, a bias toward thinking in terms of climbing ladders to success and marking nearness to perfection, even though Jung carefully differentiated between "perfection" (one-sidedly good) and "completion" (inclusive of opposites good and bad). We hear some misinformed therapists speak about "failed individuation," which suggests someone didn't pass the equivalent of the bar exam. The concern with perfection is also warned against by Buddhists, who recognize that the practice cannot be based on any kind of gaining or seen as a means to a profitable end. "Perfection" is a natural bias given the biological information we all have access to, and it also is a bias of the competitive society we inhabit.

Archetypal Psychologists do not deny the facts of biological growth, or of the evolution of beings from lesser to greater individuation. But they react to the overvaluation of the person's history and of the linear or hierarchical features of personality at the expense of the effects of chance, fate, talent, ingenuity, creativity, and the dynamic properties of the psyche which are always at work. Michael Vannoy Adams suggests that we substitute "animation by the imagination" for the term "individuation." (Young-Eisendrath and Dawson, eds., *The Cambridge Companion to Jung*, p. 113.) This phrase would tend to stress the spontaneity of becoming conscious, whereas for some "individuation" has come to carry a bias toward linear growth. We have all been nursed on hero stories, but there is a danger in looking at individuation as a hero's journey, linear and progressive. Archetypal psychologists like to say they also look at the hero myth from the point of view of the dragon.

Even though the idea is that the psyche increases in awareness in the process, the danger in seeing it as progressive is that a note of competition seeps in, a possibility of striving creeps in, a power motif peeps in, and before we know it, we are off to a heroic struggle to defeat the forces of "disindividuation" (a word I just made up), and that attitude poisons the work. We have to avoid judging others in their way of choosing to individuate or not to individuate. If we focus on a person's developmental history, we miss significant aspects of soul and its relation to death, to creativity, to restoration, to destiny. Personal history is just a small part of what moves us. We are moved by chance, opportunity, fate, luck, grace, the unconscious psyche.

Archetypal psychologies also are wary of the term "Self" when it brings up images of a solid, anthropomorphic being instead of an experience of living with vitality. If we are conditioned to a monotheistic god-image, we tend to overlook the dynamic and plural aspects of a Self. One of my children pictured God as a crystal of infinite facets, which I thought placed her in the Archetypal Psychologists' camp by age nine. (And the image could be expanded to "each facet is God, and so is the darkness in between.") Unless we can remain open to the unpredictable, we are subject to dogmatism of thought and closing off of the creative spirit.

The image of the alchemists' spiritual patron, Mercurius, as a spirit of the journey with the Self, is helpful in getting out of the linear trap. Imagine a spirit so flexible, pervasive, and ubiquitous that it can engage with anyone or anything at anytime. As Robert Grinnell says, "Mercurius as the moving energy of subjective life in the psyche appears also as a non-zonal center of unity in the total personality." (Grinnell, *Alchemy in a Modern Woman*, p. 74.) This spirit which unites but is "non-zonal" certainly relates to the quality of our current era. A uniting factor in the human personality that brings about any effective order will have to be fluid and adaptive, not fixed, rigid, or exclusive. In the story of Odysseus or Ulysses mentioned in Chapter 6, the protagonist's guide, the god Hermes, is the equivalent of the spirit Mercurius.

A fascinating illustration of the modern anti-heroic-hero in literature is James Joyce's character, Leopold Bloom, in *Ulysses*. The novel refers to Homer's story of Ulysses, and the journey of the Greek hero is the template for the anti-hero, Bloom, as he journeys through one day in Dublin. Ulysses is heroic in the brave deeds and strength of character he displays as he battles monsters, natural disasters, and evil enemies to come home to his wife, whose devotion he returns. Bloom, the modern man, also displays bravery and devotion, but it is through his anti-heroic suffering of humiliations, doubt, and acceptance of tragedy and betrayal. Where Homer's Ulysses models the superior male ego that overcomes all dangers, Bloom models the flexibility and acceptance of the survivor who maintains his human dignity and compassion in spite of being scapegoated and having his ego battered.

Individuation is not about becoming powerful, but about becoming conscious and true to ourselves. Some people in following their process do become powerful. We recognize them by their ability to take themselves lightly, their lack of arrogance, their ability to listen to others, their awareness of the common good. On the other hand, we have questions about those who have not made an effort to balance their energies, but have let power drive their process; they tend to show an inability to be flexible and to see beyond their limited egoic worldview.

None of us can evaluate the degree of another's consciousness, because consciousness is not observable. The prominent 20th century philosopher, Ludwig Wittgenstein, used the metaphor for our isolated consciousness in the image of each person having a beetle in a box, unable to see the beetle in the other's box. We may think we see evidence of awareness or lack of awareness, but we can never be sure what is being suppressed or what is temporarily not being expressed. To be completely fair, we do not know whether the current life is the only life of a particular soul, or if, as the belief in karma holds, we are given more time through reincarnation to complete our soul-making.

As a civilization, North Americans and Europeans have lived through the proud stage of social colonization globally and now have to deal with guilt, remorse, vengeance, apologies, and reconciliation, hopefully leading to empathy and collaboration with those we displaced or abandoned in the face of pogroms and genocide. Even now we face similar problems of financially and culturally oppressive colonization as we impose our products and customs onto other cultures; the results of those movements have not yet come home to roost. To be optimistic, I would like to think we are outgrowing the patriarchal mentality that led to chest-thumping of the past. Therefore, the ego-as-hero myths, admirable and exciting as they are, do not excite great aspirations in young people. Many young people are more amenable to understanding a concept of individuation that is not linear or predictable.

The evolution of the ever-popular Batman movies shows this change. Batman has evolved from super-hero to a vulnerable, imperfect humanized hero-figure. Young people are more accustomed to living with Mercurius as their guide than with a medieval crusader, or an emperor like Napoleon, or superhero model. They may better understand other possibilities, such as individuation as a circular or spiral movement. They may have a better chance of understanding the true mercurial nature of a dialogue with the Self that does not carry a power component. Mercurius is an androgynous image borrowed from the alchemists and derived from, among others, the Greek god, Hermes, the God of the Journey, of chance, of freedom from confinement, the god of mediation, resolution of contradictions, and leveling of power. It lives in the current popularity of irony, satire, and self-deprecating comedy, and in the passionate search for tolerance of "difference."

A shift in ethics reflects this trend. Whereas morality was once thought to represent a universal, timeless principle arrived at by reason, contemporary philosophers attribute moral values to our awareness of individual suffering and compassion for the distressed and maligned.

The drawing of Mercurius, Guide of Individuation, presented as frontispiece, CW 13, gives a hint about the idea of an integrated personality which contains so many paradoxes: that monstrous illustration combines many contradictory facets...cock, lion, human, serpent. Or our guide could look like the hermaphrodite globes of Plato, or the Hindu God-man in the lotus, or images of unity proceeding from the unconscious which are not affected by myth or collective stories such as the point, the circle, the quaternary, the luminous center, the magical child, and more strangely incongruous combinations. Jung meant us to see that personality is not simple and consistent. Still, it can be contained in one flexible being, and the concept of ego is not dead. Each of us has to learn to manage a more differentiated and complex world than our parents did.

That resilient ego that I referred to in a previous section recognizes that it is capable of many different faces (personae), not all of them pretty. The journey of individuation that Mercurius guides us through requires us to see that the person we decided to be at one time may not have evolved, and so, had to be replaced. Imagine a trip where you plot everything out carefully and prearrange to arrive at each hotel at a precise time; then imagine a trip where you allow yourself to meander without an exact destination, savoring the unexpected along the way. The polarities suggest an engineer partnered with a bricoleur. Most of us proceed with a less than exact map, but with an appreciation for the place of chance and irony in our human condition that enables us to enjoy the trip.

The comedian Stephen Wright says he is going to get a baby-monitor so his conscious can listen to his unconscious. It's good to know the individuation process has made it to Comedy Central! (Wright's friend sent him a picture of earth taken by satellite and inscribed, "Wish you were here.")

16

Elitism and Exceptions

*Although his cultural values have sometimes been criticized as
elitist, Jung is the great writer on individuation.*

– Andrew Samuels
The Cambridge Companion to Jung

Who individuates? "Whoever, in any age or condition, is prepared to
heed and respond to this spiritual and fundamentally human drive, is
prepared for the process of individuation." (Hart, *The Classical Jungian
School*, p. 98.)

While showing that this is a natural process, Jung also implies that
it is not actualized in all of us. He implies that most people are content
with "what lies within their reach," including meeting their spiritual
needs in the church or in community. But for others, individuation is
an inner necessity. ("The Relations Between the Ego and the Unconscious," CW 7, par. 369.)

Like many a self-improvement program, the implication is that this
process is available to a special few. Jung says in another place, it is "a
purely natural process, which may in some cases pursue its course without the knowledge or assistance of the individual, and can sometimes
forcibly accomplish itself in the face of opposition." ("On the Psychology of the Unconscious," CW 7, par. 186.) So now Jung is saying we
may not even recognize that we are chosen!

I think Jung means that sometimes, even without consciously in-
tending it, individuation is thrust upon us by circumstances. Conditions of life may force us to transform or die: losing everything; going to
prison; going into combat; getting sick; getting sober; being betrayed—
anything that causes us to change our ways, broaden our views, recognize our blind spot, and want to live differently. However, there is
no guarantee that we will follow through with conscious personality
changes, and without conscious effort there is no individuation.

There are many roads to integration and no one road is right for everybody, and the timing of the process is different for everyone. Individuation may look different at different historical and cultural ages.

My reason for writing this book is that I want people to know that individuation is available, even if you are not sophisticated in the language of psychology or philosophy. I believe that anyone who wants to can individuate if they have both 1) normal intelligence and 2) the capacity to think before reacting. For those without at least normal intelligence, I cannot say if there is some way of individuation; I would guess that there is. But if you are intractably impulsive and refuse to think before acting, you will not individuate, even if you are a genius. Still, even this is not clearly black or white. Some intelligent people have brain dysfunctions that render them impulsive, so then it is a matter of degree. Can you struggle with your impulsivity? If so, you are individuating. *Intention* is the major ingredient.

Extremely exceptional people are exceptional cases of individuation. Psychopaths are exceptional people. Seriously lacking a conscience and empathy for other humans probably prevents them from communicating with large aspects of the psyche. Their sphere of awareness may be very keen but too narrow to keep up a conversation with the unconscious. However, there is always the possibility of an opening through a dramatic turn, a revelation, or a transforming relationship. Psychoanalyst Barry Magid reports the story of a drug-addicted drag queen street hustler whose character was changed by Zen practice. (Magid, *Ending the Pursuit of Happiness*, p. 31.)

People of great talent can be possessed by their need to create at the expense of developing other aspects of personality. Samuels writes:

> Great artists whose self-realization can hardly be doubted (e.g. Mozart, Van Gogh, Gauguin) sometimes seem to have retained infantile character formation and/or psychotic traits. Were they individuated? In terms of perfection of their talent which had become amalgamated with their personalities, the answer is, yes; in terms of personal completeness and relationships, probably not. (Samuels, Shorter, and Plaut, eds., *A Critical Dictionary of Jungian Analysis*, p. 79.)

Jacobi wrote that exceptional people whose art towers far above their personal development accomplish the individuation process in their work, if it progresses and matures. The ego may remain retarded, as it is subordinated to the inspiration, and the gift develops at the expense of the human being. Sometimes confusion between artists' personal identities and their art affects their productivity, their personal relationships, and their public. For instance, they may be thought to be more mature, as their art would suggest, than they really are; then unrealistic expectations are placed upon them which create chaos in their relationships.

> The daimon of creativity has ruthlessly had its way with me. The ordinary undertakings I planned usually had the worst of it — though not always and not everywhere. (Jung, *Memories, Dreams, Reflections*, p. 358.)

I think this is especially true of writers and actors, since we judge them by their words and tend to credit them for the qualities their characters portray. One of the questions that motivated me to concentrate on the process of individuation was the enigma of the failure of famed writer James Joyce and Carl Jung to communicate when they had so much in common in ideas, lived in the same city, and functioned in the same intellectual circles. The story of their complex relationship has provoked such far-reaching issues that I now find I cannot include them all in this small space. I will simply summarize that as geniuses, they lived out such different aspects of the psyche that there was not enough time in one lifetime for them to resolve all their projections on each other.

> Great gifts are the fairest, and often the most dangerous, fruits on the tree of humanity. They hang on the weakest branches, which easily break. ("Analytical Psychology and Education," CW 17, par. 141.)

Jacobi takes up the controversy as to artists having analysis. She, Freud, and Jung agreed that if the artist cannot stand up to analysis there is something wrong with the artistry. Yet, Jacobi stipulates that the analysis must be handled with "cat's paw sensitivity." If the material from the deeper layers of the psyche is treated too rationalistically, spontaneous productivity of the symbol may be inhibited. (Jacobi, *The Way of Individuation*, pp. 28-30.) I would add that too much concern from the analyst about ego development may drain creative energy away from the source of inspiration.

If we accept the fact that individuation requires relationship with a significantly conscious other, we exclude those who for some reason cannot relate easily. This includes those who are too preoccupied to enter a close relationship, such as psychopaths, addicts, autistics, and some geniuses and saints. Although they may be advanced in some way far beyond the capacities of most of us, they may not be maturing psychologically.

By now you have some idea of what individuation entails. Here are a few areas to check:

Can you reflect? Example: "I wonder if I should choose this or not? Would it be good for me? Would it hurt anyone or anything?" "Should I have said that? Maybe I was too hasty." "I should question this opinion, even though it seems true to me."

Can you delay a reaction? Example: "I sure would like to punch her out, but I'm going to think about another way to handle this."

Can you discipline yourself? "If I drink I will be a danger behind the wheel, so I will pass on the beer and have iced tea." "When I get high I often pick a fight, so I'd rather stay sober."

Can you admit your faults? "I tend to be slovenly and need to push myself to clean up and finish assignments. I can't blame my teachers anymore."

Can you take back projections? "I think he is self-centered and hostile, but maybe I have been putting him in the same category as my previous lover, and maybe I am provoking him. I'd better check it out."

Can you combine things that seem contradictory? "They are too young, but I see they are smarter than I about this matter." "I thought I would never do this, but circumstances have changed."

Can you attend to the unconscious? Example: "Why did I dream of that again?" "What is this constant ache trying to tell me?" "Why am I so attracted to women who mistreat me?" "Why is my child so angry all the time?" "Why did I forget to pay that bill?"

Can you admit your talents? "I love to draw, but I'll never be good enough at it. Or maybe I should practice." "I don't care if they think I'm a nerd; I'm good at this, and I enjoy it."

Can you stand up against the crowd? "I'm not going to buy one just because everyone else has one."

Can you look at the bigger picture? "I wonder why other countries find this system better?" "What impact does this have on future generations?"

Can you listen to your inner voice? "I ought to help, but it's so much trouble. But helping would be the right thing."

Can you doubt your beliefs? "Science is obviously correct about evolution. But perhaps I should listen to the creationism argument and try to understand where it's coming from."

These are everyday examples of things that take some deep inner work to process carefully unless you toss them off with a snap answer.

When did you become conscious? Jung said that he was around eleven when he said to himself, "I am myself now." I remember realizing at some childhood juncture that I would be this same person for a lifetime. I also remember trying to imagine eternity. It filled me with frustration and wonder, which I now see as a longing for the divine.

Some of us remember such invitations from the psyche to pursue awareness that then we ignored. We may remember when we decided to stop being ourselves and conform to the crowd...or the opposite, when we decided to separate from the crowd and drop out. Or we may have given up doing something we loved in order to take the path of least resistance. Or we stopped wondering because we became too confused and couldn't find an answer to a conflict.

Nietzsche's "Übermensche" and Jung's Self have invited comparisons. Both imply a process of self-examination that is difficult for the average person to accomplish. Both Jung and Nietzsche can be interpreted as elitists in their promotion of separation from a herd-mentality. Nietzsche, however, draws conclusions about how the powerfully self-realized individual functions in society that has very different effects from Jung's vision. Briefly stated, for Jung there must be a balance between the social persona an individual adopts and her/his inner values and vocation, whereas Nietzsche envisions a society dominated by the most powerful. A thorough exploration of the similarities and differences in Jung's and Nietzsche's approaches to elitism is found in *Nietzsche and Jung*, by Lucy Huskinson.

In conclusion, if you have read this far, you can individuate.

He's a real Nowhere Man,
Sitting in his Nowhere Land,
Making all his nowhere plans for nobody.
Doesn't have a point of view,
Knows not where he's going to,
Isn't he a bit like you and me?

... He's as blind as he can be,
Just sees what he wants to see
Nowhere Man can you see me at all?

Nowhere Man, please listen,
You don't know what you're missing
Nowhere Man, the world is at your command.

–John Lennon and Paul McCartney

17

Beyond the Depressive Position

After Freud developed his observation that a person moves through oral, anal, and phallic stages in the process of becoming a functional adolescent and adult, his followers continued to refine his theory about the early stages of infancy. In coming to their conclusions they observed their own children and also the dreams, memories, symptoms, and fantasies of their adult patients. They also projected their desires and adult imagination into theories about what happens in the minds of infants.

One prominent Freudian, Melanie Klein, supposed that infants do not come into the world secure and placid about their survival. Even with a good parent, an infant goes through an anxious stage that only is overcome when the infant has consistent care and attention and is able to establish trust in its survival, according to Klein. This initial stage of utter dependence and fusion with its environment (particularly mother) Klein called the "paranoid position," and it was expected to be resolved in the first few months of life. It was assumed that adults who were suspicious and cynical had not been sufficiently secured in their parents' love during that early stage and did not progress to the next developmental stage of more psychological security called the "depressive position."

If the paranoid stage was satisfactorily maneuvered, Klein thought, the infant came to recognize and trust the parent and to depend on having its needs met. The infant was now able to have an experience of "other" and of being a separate being. A loving bond was formed between infant and parent. Now the child became vulnerable to the inconsistency of attention that is part of every parent-child relationship and is inevitable, as all parents have lapses of attention to the infant due to conditions such as illness, preoccupation with problems and other children to care for, and unavoidable absences, and the infant does not get its needs attended to comfortably some of the time. This stage Klein called the "depressive position"; it is characterized by the ability to form loving relationships throughout life, but periods of depression result when the relationships fail to satisfy. It was implied that all well-adapted adults remain in the depressive position, since all of us remain vulnerable to mistakes and failures in relationship.

This differs from the observations of Jungian analyst Michael Fordham and others, but I mention Klein's theory because it is popular among developmental psychologists and lends itself to understanding the changing attitudes to the transpersonal which we are going to look at now.

Depression is a widespread problem and somewhat of a mystery. Most psychotherapists believe that manic-depression, also known as bipolar-disorder, has a strong genetic component and requires medication to manage the mood swings it creates. There are other kinds of depression (not to be confused with conscious mourning), with various causes, provocations, and prognoses. The effects of depression range from sad moods, "the blues," to paralyzing degrees of despair and fear. All depression creates physiological reactions in the body, but the origin of the depression can be physical or psychological. One physiological factor is thought to be the prolonged presence of high levels of stress hormones produced because of a chronic threat, real or perceived.

In depression we meet an intense body-psyche mystery, as we do not know how much of our reaction to depressive events is learned behavior—which can be changed through changing thoughts, allowing repressed feelings to be felt, learning new habits of living and relating, or taking better care of ourselves—and how much persists through genetic neurohormonal circuitry.

One hypothesis about some depressions is that they are messages from the Self urging us to transform. William James experienced depression and wrote movingly about a variety of kinds of melancholy from passive joylessness to powerful dread and panic. James noted how often the condition led to a transformation in the whole experience of reality. The sufferer is forced to question life's significance and the meaning of having been visited with something out of her or his control. Just as we are visited by the passion of love, we can be "gifted" with fear, dread, or jealousy and find our world drained of color.

> Gifts, either of the flesh or of the spirit; and the spirit bloweth where it listeth. (James, *Varieties of Religious Experience*.)

Recently the concept of a transcendent stage, always accepted by Jungian psychologists, has emerged in Freudian thought. In this stage, though life disappoints and fails to gratify our expectations, the reaction of depression has been outgrown. In depression we tend to feel sorry for ourselves and perhaps guilty for what has happened to us. This is a natural reaction to disappointment. But it is not inevitable. There comes a time in the life of a person who has learned reflection and acquired the ability to take back projections when adversity is seen as another vicissitude of life to be experienced and moved through.

Many adults cannot reach this transcendent level of maturity because of emotional deprivation suffered in early life; psychotherapy can be of help for such persons by creating an environment where new emotional experiences are possible and the maturation process is accelerated. It is as if a door to the attitudes that fuel depression has been closed, and space is always open for the new. We have then moved beyond Klein's "depressive condition" and into the transcendent phase of personality development. This is not to say that it is a permanent state, for, with enough stress, unpredictable reactions and regression can happen.

We project expectations and images on conditions...being rich, being strong, being independent, being married, being employed, and so on, and when we fail to meet those conditions, we may feel devastated. Sometimes our projections are on other people: that they will always love us, they will support us, they will live long, they will not get angry, and so on, and when those disappoint, we are devastated.

I do not imply that we should repress or suppress our disappointment, or force ourselves to "always look on the bright side of life" as in the silly crucifixion scene in Monty Python's classic film, "The Life of Brian." Usually one can learn to embrace and transcend disappointment. Transcending psychological pain occurs organically, without effort, except the effort of having practiced being reflective. Some achieve the ability to transcend pain at an early age, others only after many depressing experiences have been suffered through. Transcending psychological pain is the goal of some meditation regimes.

Transcendence is not individuation, but is an aspect of individuation. Mindfulness does not guarantee that one can see clearly into complexes and unconscious motives, as we attempt to do in individuation. To the extent that we can transcend complexes and move beyond depression, mindfulness is helpful.

One view of depression suggests that there are some who are genetically programmed to experience recurrent depression, regardless of their attitudes and lifestyles. This conclusion, supported by drug companies, is debatable and requires more research. At this point research by non-pharmaceutical companies indicates that drugs do significantly improve manic-depressive and schizophrenic disorders, but they are not unequivocally helpful for other kinds of depression in the long term. (Horgan, "Why Freud Isn't Dead," pp. 106-111.)

In the case of depression that is a result of the effect of stress hormones on the system, though none of us can control the amount of stress we are subjected to, we do have some choice about how to meet stressors. Studies of early infant-parent interaction show that insecure attachment in infancy makes one more vulnerable to stress and more likely to suffer post-traumatic stress disorder later. (Schore, "The Effect of Early Relational Trauma on Right Brain Development," 2001.) We can see this as confirming the inevitability toward depression in those who have had poor experiences in early life. But if the human system is vulnerable to psychological features in early infancy, this implies that there is a psychological solution to the problem as well. It has been shown that the relationship between therapist and patient is capable of changing neuronal patterns, including the tendency to depression, as well as the tendency to get into depressing situations. A study reported in the *Journal of the American Medical Association* concluded, after compiling thousands of research studies, that long-term-psychodynamic-psychotherapy is significantly more effective than short-term therapy for complex mental disorders (because of the therapeutic relationship). (Leichsenring, "Effectiveness of LTPP," pp. 1551-1565.)

The great tragedies in opera—*Tosca, Tristan and Isolde, Aida*, for example; in literature—*Hamlet, Oedipus, Anna Karenina*, and so on; in popular movies and song, in stories that we gravitate to in the news and gossip columns, all prepare us to deal with loss. So powerful is the tragedy of loss that every religion, every philosophy, every art form and mythology holds tragedy and loss as a major theme. As we learn to accept losses, so it is possible for some people to learn to overcome the tendency toward depression. The state of equanimity required to do so has been attained by some people, as described throughout the ages by persons exposed to extreme trauma and privation—some who suffered abandonment in childhood, prisoners of war, holocaust victims, refugees, the severely handicapped. Furthermore, there is growing support for the notion that the individuation process, under ideal conditions, can proceed to a state of consistent peace of soul and capacity to unite with humanity in all its tragic particularities, as well as with an experience of the divine in all its glory. As each of us attempts to deal with loss, there is at least implied in these cultural expressions the assumption that loss must be accepted, if not embraced and welcomed—that there is an "other side" to melancholy, and one must go through suffering to get there. And there reside wisdom and courage.

An exception to this assumption is our current medical model which encourages the repression of feelings of loss through anti-depressants. Some physicians believe that depression is likely to recur, and with each recurrence become more onerous. If it is treated with medication at the first appearance, they believe, the brain is less vulnerable to the chemical changes that bring on depression. There is abundant evidence that some depressions and bipolar disorders are genetically programmed aberrations of chemical functions which respond dramatically to medication, which may make the difference between a life of chaos and unpredictability and a more satisfying equilibrium.

Whether with pharmacology we are on the cusp of something that will make all of our previous wisdom obsolete, no one can say. It is too soon to know what we are preparing our coming generations to be. Nor do we know what they will be asked to live through. In the meantime, each of us must track our own experiences to decide how we will handle loss and the question of medication for ourselves. But we should keep in mind that worlds of experience and generations of wisdom tell us that suffering is to be borne if it is to lead to transformation and knowledge.

Mathematician John Nash, whose life was the subject of the movie, "A Beautiful Mind," in his address to the American Psychiatric Association in 2007, asked: "Does nature have a purpose in producing mental disorders, like depression and schizophrenia? Can there be an evolutionary purpose in these conditions which we do not have enough information to comprehend at this stage of human development?"

My good friend who has suffered serious depressions wrote:

> Depression might be understood as the descent of the
> psyche preparatory to spiritual gnosis. William James wrote,
> "The completest religions...seem to be those in which the
> pessimistic elements are best developed ... essentially reli-
> gions of deliverance: that man must die to an unreal life
> before he can be born into the real life." Depression may
> not be accidental but teleological, a stage in a universal
> transformation leading to enlightenment. (Dr. B., in Mc-
> Neely, *Walking the Crooked Mile*, p. 165.)

Professor David Miller notes that the neurotic feeling of "nothingness" is not the same "nothingness" about which the religious are speaking. The psychological symptom which feels like nothing is something
negative. Miller writes:

> If the experience is not nothing, why then does it present
> itself as if it were nothing? Why do I say that I am nothing
> when I am not, when I am in fact full of negative some-
> thing? Why do I say that my life is empty when in fact it
> is full of what seems like substantial darkness? What is the
> teleology of this error, this mistaken utterance? What is
> the psyche's autonomous "purpose" in this "self-presenta-
> tion"? (Miller, *Nothing Almost Sees Miracles! Self and No-Self
> in Psychology and Religion*, pp. 16-17.)

Miller wonders if there is a clue to the answer in the mystical tradition:

> ... my experience of so-called "nothingness" may be an
> initiation into the deeper "no-thingness" which apophatic
> religious experience calls (for lack of a word) "God." It is
> an invitation to deepen what the "I" takes to be the "noth-
> ingness," to go into it more thoroughly than to cure it or
> to attempt (vainly) to be rid of it. Could it be that the epi-
> demic psychological depression in North America may be
> a concealed wish for spirituality? ...our sense of worthless-
> ness and hopelessness might be experienced as "positive,"
> leading to "a new synthesis," "purposeful," "a precious
> possession," and even our "best friend." (Miller, *Nothing
> Almost Sees Miracles! Self and No-Self in Psychology and Reli-
> gion*, pp. 16-17.)

Such is life
Seven times down
Eight times up.

–Japanese poem (quoted in Watts, *The Way of Zen*, p. 86.)

18

Transcendent Traditions: A New Myth

The day will come when, after harnessing space, the winds, the tides and gravitation, we shall harness for God the energies of love. And on that day, for the second time in the history of the world, we shall have discovered fire.

— Michael Reagan, *The Hand of God*

There are many schools of psychological and/or spiritual development. One essential feature that distinguishes Jung's way of individuation from other ways is "shadow work." Let us look at what that entails.

Jung belongs to a large number of visionaries who realized that humanity in the modern world needed psychological and spiritual renewal. Not that Jung claimed to start a spiritual group movement. He tried to show a way for individuals to step back from a darkly materialistic age and find solace in their own gifts from the unconscious. But he also realized that the fear that seizes us when faced with the unknown keeps us from wanting to know the unconscious and irrational factors in ourselves, even our spiritual dimensions.

When I was a child I heard that Jesus and Mary sometimes appeared to people in visions, as happened to Bernadette of Lourdes. The thought of being visited by a divine being terrified me so, that I prayed to Jesus and Mary to please not choose to come to me. I suppose I knew intuitively that my ego could not withstand such an infusion of psychic energy. Many people experience a similar terror in the presence of a psychotic person, or the first time they attend a religious ceremony at which some people give in to spiritual ecstasy and lose consciousness. It is hard to give up ego-control.

Jung's special contribution to the effort to renew spiritual life was his insight into the unconscious complexes that interfere with our most sincere plans and intentions. The most devout and altruistic of us are not exempt from being undermined and deceived from within. Jung was insistent that our first responsibility was to clear up any one-sided fixations of our own unexamined evils onto others of different beliefs, traditions, ethnicities, and personality types. In Jungian terms we call this working on becoming aware of our "Shadow."

Many spiritual movements ignore the importance of this psychological fact and end in power struggles, divisive squabbles over details, and split-loyalties between members. This is why Jungians place so much importance on clearly individual psychological work while searching for spiritual nourishment. Unless we deal with our inner conflicts, we thrust them into any group efforts we attempt. They color and pollute our religious institutions.

It is possible for a person to acquire a dominant spiritual life and still remain emotionally infantile, unable to negotiate psychological pitfalls. Jung's efforts were to help us secure a solid relationship with physical and social reality as well as spiritual reality. Power-hungry gurus, abusive priests, charlatan preachers, extravagant church funds, censors of books and information-sources by which institutions protect their authority are ways people's personal complexes poison their spirituality.

Edward Edinger wrote that Jung's work, which Edinger calls a "new myth," has the capacity to unite all the religions of the world. It is not one more religious myth in competition with all the others; rather, it elucidates every other religion:

> The new myth can be understood and lived within one
> of the great religious communities such as Catholic Chris-
> tianity, Protestant Christianity, Judaism, Buddhism, etc.,
> or in some new community yet to be created, or by in-
> dividuals without specific community connections.... For
> the first time in history we now have an understanding of
> man so comprehensive and fundamental that it can be the
> basis for a unification of the world — first religiously and
> culturally and, in time, politically. When enough individu-
> als are carriers of the "consciousness of wholeness," the
> world itself will become whole. (Edinger, *The Creation of
> Consciousness*, p. 32.)

Shadow work is the leveler of all factions. Marvin Spiegelman, an analyst who has written autobiographical accounts of his relationship to Jung and religion, had a dream as a youth which pertains to this possibility of unity as expressed by Edinger as well as by others, such as the philosopher, Teilhard de Chardin. The dream was that *three wise men, a Jewish rabbi, a Catholic priest, and a Buddhist priest, were coming to visit a new divine child.* The dream led him to believe that some new way of approaching the God-image is emerging in the psyche. He might have taken it to mean that this was happening in him as a single, personal experience, but he later learned that Jung was having the same idea. Here is what Spiegelman says about his dream:

> This newer experience of the divine is to be found in a reconciliation among the religions of the world and their ability to worship and connect with a new content. I think that this content, which independently emerged both in Jung and others, is a kind of psycho-religious attitude, if one can use such a word. The qualities of this attitude are: the divine transcends us all; there are many paths to it, all of which have truth or are part of a whole; all paths are worthy, none better than others; none need be transcended; all religions find their origin in the nature of the soul itself and how the divine manifests therein. This is surely a Hindu view, a Buddhist view, a Jewish view, a Christian view, but only for some sects or branches of each one.... There seems to be more expectation or desire that the new divine child, "savior," is to appear outside ourselves rather than inside. Thus there is the awaited Messiah, Second Coming, the fulfillment of prophecy, and in a more modern vein, the sense that our earth will encounter consciousness from other planets or stars. They are probably right, but it is Jung's—and Buddhism's—gift to us to look for that emergence from within our own souls. So we all will have a lot to do with ourselves until that outer Buddha, Christ, Messiah, appears. God willing, it will be synchronistic. It is noted in Jewish lore, that when every Jew observes Shabbat, the Messiah will appear. To extrapolate, when all of us are in tune with the Divine Presence, HE / SHE / IT will manifest among us all. (Spiegelman and Miyuki, *Buddhism and Jungian Psychology*, pp. 188-189.)

This optimistic picture seems far from possible in this age of religious strife, holy wars, and philosophical attacks on a principle of unity. But throughout history there have been men like Jung, Edinger, and Spiegelman who stand for the power of the uniting principle to transform what often appears doomed: life in the universe, and at least, the life of the soul.

Jung was not in the business of starting a new religion. Born into a Christian worldview, he was inquiring into why religion, particularly Christianity, his tradition, was not meaningful to many who called themselves Christian in name only. Their connection to their religion seemed dead, but they carried on as if they still believed what they were doing. In his research into the problem, he discovered that the religious component of psyche is deep and universal. Beneath layers of conscious material is a center, like a fountain of psychic energy, which enlivens the mind and heart and asks to be honored. It makes itself known to us through symbols which attract us and touch us emotionally. He called it the Self and realized that our notions of God spring from that center of energy.

When we are in touch with that center, we understand the religious experience. It comes alive with awe, but it may or may not resonate to the usual religious symbols; it gives us a personal relationship with a divinity or divinities that may or may not include our known institutional symbols, pictures, stories or formal rituals to which we are accustomed. The new myth has appeal to atheists and all who experience a need for integrity without a specific god-image.

For Jung the *way* that we express religious wonder was not the point. The point is to experience the deepest layers of the unconscious, or Self, where our divinity makes itself known. This is dangerous, however, because we can transfer the energy from the source to our own aggrandizement. Without humility, humankind can become so selfish that we can destroy our civilization and planet. Atheism is not in itself destructive. Many atheists are humanists who put the dignity of man above their own needs and achieve a lifestyle that is respectful and compassionate. But without the leaven of humility and gratitude toward something beyond the personal, Jung feared we would become victims of power hunger, with the power that belonged to the Self transferred to our egos. This raises the issue of the basic goodness of human beings. Was Jung right? Do we need a deep relationship to the transcendent layer of psyche to evolve morally, or can we do it from a purely human perspective and from the layer of conscious ego?

Philosopher Simone Weil thought that without a concept of the supernatural, human relationships would be dominated by the powerful, not by mutual consent. What is natural is for humans to assert themselves whenever possible, and if our conception of God is of a commanding being who favors one side over another and uses his power to cause events, then any atrocity can be committed in the name of such a god. Weil calls such religions false. A true religion is one which holds supernatural values and inspires one to practice supernatural degrees of justice, friendship, and so on. For example, one treats as equals those who are below him in strength and status and does not take advantage to accumulate power. (Morgan, *Weaving the World: Simone Weil on Science, Mathematics, and Love.*)

Spiritual leaders as well as atheists risk assuming the power of the Self for their own aggrandizement. The power exuded by a charismatic leader attracts followers who need the charge, so the inflation of the leader continues to be fed. Jung's injunction to continually look at our shadow prevents inflation and encourages humility.

Jung suggested that the way humankind can honor the religious instinct without being pulled apart and destroyed by it is to maintain a dialogue with that inner source from which all religions spring:

> This is a thought that goes beyond the Christian world of ideas and involves a mystery consummated in and through man. It is as though the drama of Christ's life were, from now on, located in man as its living carrier. As a result of this shift, the events formulated in dogma are brought within range of psychological experience and become recognizable in the process of individuation. ("Mysterium Coniunctionis," CW 14, par. 650.)

How do we carry this particularly Christian drama in a way that feels alive? Christian mystics live out Jung's thought that the birth of God in the human soul is a constantly repeated event, an ongoing act of creation. Jungian psychoanalyst John Dourley says:

> The soul which is in some sense the creature of God is needed by God to mediate God's energies to consciousness... God's birth in the soul... Mary's virgin birth is a symbol for processes of psychological and spiritual maturation which are universal and true of both genders... God seeks to be born again and again in the soul. (Dourley, *A Strategy for a Loss of Faith*, p. 125.)

Such an attitude does not apply only to Christians. As Edinger explains: "We are in a position to begin to understand scientifically, and generally, the psychological entities that generate religions." (Edinger, *Science of the Soul*, p. 58.) Because we are on such an edge of self-destruction, Jung called this time in human development "a moment of deadliest peril." ("The Archetypes and the Collective Unconscious," CW 9i, par. 217.) Jung's hope was that enough people would encounter the Greater Personality to effectively inoculate the culture against inflation as atheism and inflation as religious fanaticism.

"The universe begins to look more like a great thought than a great machine," said Sir James Jeans. (Jeans, quoted in Wilbur, *Quantum Questions*, p. 133.)

19

Transcendent Traditions: Jung and Buddhism

Jung became acquainted with Buddhism through studying Schopenhauer, who had incorporated Buddhist thought into his philosophical system. Buddhism, especially Japanese Buddhism under the influence of Shintoism, as generally understood, does not worship a god and comes closest of the spiritual traditions, in my opinion, to the Jungian way of life. Buddhism places responsibility on our own efforts to achieve the spiritual awakening that transcends suffering and death. Unlike most religions, it encourages self-reflection in a way closest to the Jungian psychological dimension. In some forms it is not contradictory to practicing a religion. Buddhism and Christianity have been shown to be compatible. In holding compassion as the greatest value, Buddhism is like most great religions.

What began as a small religious community in northern India grew into a global religious tradition with many different beliefs and figures of worship. Buddhism cannot be generalized as one system of belief. Many paths lead to the central core of no-self. Buddhism teaches that our identity as a personal self is an illusion, and the larger Self cannot be identified because it is no-thing. In working through the desires that cause our suffering, we look not just at what causes and frustrates those desires, but at how we experience the being (ego identity) doing the desiring. We stop identifying ourselves with the suffering, and we step aside and watch our suffering. This "watching" and "listening to" is not repressing or denying the suffering; it is reflecting. In this way it describes the individuation process. It is said that Buddha holds a mirror to us.

The Christian mystic, Meister Eckhart, a Dominican monk, claimed that disinterested attachment is higher than love in relationship to the divine. This is a profound but difficult statement to comprehend, and it can only be experienced when, as Eckhart describes, the soul has received the Godhead in a nothingness annihilating all distinctions between God and herself. Jung links Eckhart with the satori experience of the Zen tradition, because both experience the transcendent layer of the psyche directly, without anyone or anything mediating it. (Dourley, *A Strategy for a Loss of Faith*, pp. 120-126.)

While Jung from his European background stressed the importance of images in knowing the Self, Buddhism recognizes a layer of psychic being beyond images, the serene and eternal absence of desire in any form. It teaches us the psychic dimension beyond urgency, before any energy patterns (archetypes) emerge to motivate creation. This psychic dimension is the stillness that mystics of all religions come to know. Jung intuited that this is a dimension of psyche, a creative energy within the human unconscious that manifests as religious experience. It could be called the Godhead or Pleroma that precedes the Creator God.

Jung explored all the Eastern religions but warned that the ways of meditation of the East were not appropriate for the Western person. He felt that Eastern spirituality was prepared by generations of introversion to descend into "nameless non-being," but that Westerners have been immersed in extroversion and need to open up to the unconscious and the fantasies it brings up, not move away from our fantasies in meditation. But since then, as Spiegelman notes, many Westerners have submitted to Eastern disciplines, and though some have dropped out or used them bizarrely, many have been able to immerse themselves in Eastern techniques and viewpoints without problems and with the benefits of an expansion of consciousness. (Spiegelman and Miyuki, *Buddhism and Jungian Psychology*, p. ii.) In this twenty-first century, Westerners are capable of reaching the deepest dimensions of the psyche that lie beyond the source of archetypal energies.

A Jungian Buddhist writes:

> One of the most basic aspects of the foundational Western Psychic Tree, as I understand it, is the verse from Exodus that reveals the Divine Name. "God said to Moses, 'I am he who is.'" (Exodus 3:14.) The god of Moses is. He has being. My own Eastern Evolutionary Tree is very different. In Japan, the beginning of all that exists is not an Ultimate Being, but Great Emptiness. This emptiness is not the opposite of being, not nothingness or a sterile void. Rather it is a ground of emptiness that is pregnant with possibility and full of potential. In the East, everything begins with this empty non-being that, nonetheless, can take on form

and become visible. (Kazuhiko Higuchi, in Marlan, *Archetypal Psychologies*, p. 491.)

Jungian analyst Mokusen Miyuki explains that, contrary to popular opinion, the meditative practices of Eastern religions are not meant to dissolve the ego but to make the ego, as Jung suggests, "Self-centric." In the service of the Self, the ego is replenished by assimilating the contents of the unconscious, so that it becomes enriched and strengthened. Miyuki says:

> Psychologically viewed, the Buddhist emphasis on further awakening refers to this constant process of growth and development of the ego. Thus understood, the essential feature of Buddhism does not consist in ego-dissolution but, rather, in ego enrichment through the integration of the unconscious. (Spiegelman and Miyuki, *Buddhism and Jungian Psychology*, p. 173.)

Another who has written clearly on this issue of the Eastern and Western psyche and how Buddhism and depth psychology work together is psychoanalyst Mark Epstein. Epstein notes that most Westerners begin meditation from an experience of alienation due to early separation from the family group; Easterners begin from an experience of enmeshment in the family group. This makes Westerners more likely to suffer from feelings of unworthiness and longing for belonging, and Easterners to suffer from longing for escape from the collective and guilt about that. (Epstein, *Thoughts Without a Thinker*, pp. 178-180.)

Epstein explains that Buddhism stresses the inherent impossibility of figuring out who or what we are, with or without "good enough mothering," and Buddhists resolve the dilemma by encouraging not knowing. "Insight arises best when the thinker's existence is no longer necessary." (Epstein, *Thoughts Without a Thinker*, p. 222.)

Epstein uses this example of a Buddhist exercise to illustrate the difference in Eastern and Western attitudes: To cultivate compassion, a Tibetan Buddhist guided meditation asked meditators to imagine all beings as mother:

> Since cyclic existence is beginningless... all beings have, at some time or another, been in every possible relationship to one another. Thus, all beings have been both enemies and friends, and it is only through the impact of greed, hatred and ignorance that the benevolent relationships

have soured. The particular exercise involves recognizing all beings as our mothers—feeling their kindness, developing the desire to repay their kindness, feeling love for them because of their potential for this kindness, and developing the wish that they be freed from suffering and its causes. The psychic root of this practice is the unambivalent love that the Tibetan population is able to summon for their own mothers.

Epstein describes how this exercise for some Westerners was disastrous because their relationships with their mothers were so conflicted. "When the child's temperament runs counter to the parent's or when the parent's ambitions for the child obscure who the child actually is, the family unit easily becomes an alienating or claustrophobic environment in which the child must hide out from the very beings toward whom she is most needy." When asked about this exercise about mothers, a Tibetan master said, "Oh no, not for Westerners. I always tell them like grandmother or grandfather." (Epstein, *Thoughts Without a Thinker*, pp. 75-76.)

Claire Douglas lists several similarities between Jung and Eastern philosophy. She states that both: validate the idea of the unconscious and give further insight into it; stress the importance of inner life; value completion rather than perfection; have a concept of psychic integration (individuation); and seek a way beyond the opposites through balance and harmony. Also, the paths of self-discipline and self-realization taught by Eastern philosophy through the withdrawal of projections and through yoga, meditation, and introspection are similar to the deep analytic process. (Young-Eisendrath and Dawson, eds., *The Cambridge Companion to Jung*, p. 29.)

Psychoanalyst Polly Young-Eisendrath has promoted dialogues between Western psychotherapists and Japanese Zen Buddhists. She notes that the Japanese bring assumptions to their understanding of the psyche which are different from those of Westerners, even if the latter practice some form of Buddhism. It is described as a different perspective on the so-called dualities, such as mind-body, individual-group, and life-death. The Japanese do not experience a split between these dualities as do most educated people in Europe and America. (In chapter 14 on world cultures, we noted this difference in the Cartesian effects on thought in the West since the period in philosophy known as the Enlightenment.) Westerners are often made uncomfortable by the principles of Buddhism, which sees these matters differently and can accept concepts such as the life-death continuum without great struggle. And the Japanese have to stretch their perspectives to take in a psychotherapeutic focus that places importance on personal knowledge and self-concern without experiencing shame. These differences in perspective, though deep and difficult to overcome, can be lifted. (Young-Eisendrath and Muramoto, eds., *Awakening and Insight: Zen Buddhism and Psychotherapy,* pp. 6-7.)

There is a place in the psyche where these sorts of differences disappear and a union of perspectives of can be found.

> Esoteric mysticism may become a political and religious necessity because of the more universal empathy it carries. (Dourley, "In the End It All Comes to Nothing: The Basis of Identity in Non-Identity," Lecture given at The International Association for Jungian Studies, p. 7.)

O look in the mirror,
  O look in your distress,
Life remains a blessing
  Although you cannot bless.

O stand, stand at the window
  As the tears scald and start;
You shall love your crooked neighbor
  With your crooked heart.

– W. H. Auden
from "As I Walked Out One Evening"

20

Other Transcendent Traditions

The False God changes suffering into violence;
The True God changes violence into suffering.

–Simone Weil, *Gravity and Grace*

I singled out Buddhism to compare with Jungian individuation because it is being so thoroughly studied in both Eastern and Western cultures. Equally interesting are the relationships of individuation to other methods of promoting spiritual awareness, the major religions and their special sects, such as Islam's Sufism, as well as movements like Judaism's Kabbalists, Theosophy, Anthroposophy, the Spiritual Exercises of Ignatius, Mystery Schools, the teachings of Gurdjieff, Transcendentalism, and so on. Many of these traditions practice a way of speaking with the unconscious that is similar to Jung's Active Imagination. However, their practices do not include working out unconscious complexes, that is, shadow work.

Jung was touched by many of these traditions because he explored them as aspects of unconscious influence and evidence of archetypal patterns in the human psyche. Jung's attention to occult practices, mysticism, astrology, alchemy, UFOs, synchronicity, and divination made it easy for New Age seekers to claim him as their own.

However, the way of individuation cannot be identified with the New Age movement; they are inherently different, as Jungian psychoanalyst Don Williams has clarified by detailing the history of "New Thought" and "New Age" in an online essay. The precursor to New Age spirituality was the New Thought movement of the 1860s. A leader was Phineas Quimby, who experimented in mesmerism. Disease was considered a thought that we believe. He inspired Christian Scientism, Norman Vincent Peale (*The Power of Positive Thinking*), and Helen Schucman (*A Course in Miracles*). New Thought influenced the move away from the purely somatic view of emotional disorders, and toward the concept of psychotherapy.

Williams points out that legitimate psychotherapists tried to distinguish themselves from faith healers and charlatans who disregard medical science. Jung understood the passion behind these movements as due to psychic energy which could no longer be invested in obsolete religious forms. (Williams cites resources—see Part III.) Related to this subject is a wealth of material on positive psychology (attributed to Martin Seligman) and the popularity of the "happiness principle." Sociological and neuroscientific research about what makes us happy abounds. The debate is too vast to cover here, but generally, absorption in meaningful projects is regarded by many people as the most gratifying of experiences.

To distinguish between New Age movements (like "The Secret," or the "Course in Miracles") and the individuation process, Williams calls attention to a fundamental New Age belief in personal responsibility for creating reality by our thoughts. Although we may listen to the unconscious and thereby reduce some problems arising from inattention, Jung believed we are never in complete control of our thoughts.

Neither do we have the power to cure our illnesses through thought, manipulate our destiny, wish ourselves into wealth, and rise above unintended psychological problems and complexes. We might work to mitigate the effects of our character faults and succeed to the point that we attain inner peace by accepting our own evil tendencies, but we never claim that that is a matter of pure wish, will power, or moral superiority. To do so would mean attributing the power of the Self to ourselves, becoming inflated and in danger of becoming unrealistically arrogant or narcissistic. In addition, we understand the Self as a transcendent mystery, not a source of good will to those who seek its favor.

Analyst Janet Dallett points out that New Age thought is not new but is caught up in Victorianism's concern with respectability and one-sided religiosity that cast evil into the unconscious. "This perspective promotes an illusory transcendence by encouraging repression and denial of unpleasant facts and emotions." (Dallett, *Saturday's Child: Encounters with the Dark Gods*, p. 15.)

Jung did not see himself as a prophet (as many spiritualists do); he meant to be a scientific observer who did not disregard medical science and the accumulated knowledge from the past and who was curious about all psychic contents. He also did not want a cult following, which New Agers are inclined to create. Jungians do not see Jung as a superhuman and faultless leader but as a very intelligent man who was far from perfect or saintly, but whose ideas were ahead of his culture and time.

Jung's process of individuation stresses what these New Age movements lack: know your shadow, respect your limitations, and recognize how easy ego-inflation can be. There are many movements which promise personality transformation which cannot be called religions, but which possibly, for some people, answer the need that Jung identified as spiritual. The Positive Psychology movement promotes good mental health by focusing on the positive, much like the "Power of Positive Thinking" of Norman Vincent Peale, the Transactional Analysis (better known as "I'm O.K., You're O.K."), and the "Purposeful Life" of the Evangelical Christians. All of these can be good and useful ways of organizing a life, but they carry a danger of becoming unbalanced regarding real threats, inner and outer. Like any oversimplified approach to problem solving, it may become easier to rush to judgment on the positive side than to respond to nuances. A lot of psychological truth is not clearly positive or negative, but complicated.

All institutionalized religions and spiritual movements can and have been exploited at times by power-hungry factions and fundamentalist ideologues. In addition, power factions exploit the spiritual needs of people to earn fame and make a profit. It is hard to judge the many current trends, like Scientology, that promise a kind of transcendence. I am not in a position to judge such groups without personal experience, but my impression is that they differ from authentic spirituality in that they appear to be rewarding an image of perfection, not expanded multi-dimensional consciousness. Often they appear to be promoting the profit motive, both in money and correctness of being, but not promoting a relationship to the integrating center of the psyche.

The way of consciousness asks that we accept our own imperfections, not condemn them. Becoming more conscious of our tendency to project what we feel to be unacceptable (our shadow) onto others offers some possibility of changing the way that religious groups relate to each other. If we demean the clothing or rituals of other religions (for example, traditions such as shouting, keeping silence, ecstatic dancing, or dietary laws) as unacceptable ways of worship, we need to look deeply into ourselves and examine the source of our judgments. We might even make an effort to understand them.

All religions have in common the fundamental principles of belief in the possibility of unity and universal love. As human, finite enterprises, they may fall short of carrying out those principles, but because they open us to awareness of those principles, they deserve respect. As the Whitman poem in Chapter 4 suggests, loving connections cut through philosophical fog. The passionate lovers, the ecstatic poets from Rumi and Hafiz to John Lennon and Maya Angelou, the Bhakti yogis and first-responders, the Sufi dancers and the Tangoers, the participants in ancient Dionysian festivals and modern Olympic Games: in each of these, the fire of life burns bright.

In contrast to the "disinterested attachment" attained by some mystics, the expressions of love that resonate in religious images of Sophia-Wisdom, the all-pervasive Great Spirit and Sacred Heart, the Sacred Marriage, and the bliss of nirvana remind us of our human heritage. In these poetic spiritual images we do not meet concerns about the nature of being or non-being, nor questions of dogma or rightness/wrongness, but only of immersion in awe and loving wonder. All reason and contradictions are consumed in the flame of devotion. In this way they may be judged as psychologically one-sided, but recognizing the depth of the psyche; they may also be seen as extending beyond the archetypal realm into pure oneness with the divine. Jung's psychology supports a spiritual dimension of life. It is no small thing that Jung, in the final years of a long life, gave us an example by ending his autobiography with an homage to Love. (See Part III, "Lagniappe," Chapter 20.)

21

A Question of Endpoints

The final mystery is oneself. When one has weighed the sun in the balance, and measured the steps of the moon, and mapped out the seven heavens star by star, there still remains oneself. Who can calculate the orbit of his own soul?

.– Oscar Wilde, "De Profundis"

We began with a question of principles, and we end with a question of endpoints. In human experience there are no clear-cut endpoints. Even death can be seen as a process of changing states, the disintegration of some factors as new states continue to emerge. So in speaking about psychological growth, we are not likely to find any final goals.

Andrew Samuels articulates the possibility of seeing individuation as having a goal (the Holy Grail), or seeing the process itself as the goal or grail. It was easier to project a goal-setting function onto the Self in the last century. These days it is easier to think in terms of an unpredictable journey than an endpoint. The question of spiritual or mystical summons is not ruled out, however, for some of us.

Individuation may be both a natural psychological development and a spiritual calling. As a psychological process, the spiritual may not call everyone; but as a spiritual calling, the psychological must be included. It cannot be overlooked, or else it is not individuation. In individuation, psychological awareness is a necessity; spiritual awareness a choice.

So although it no longer is appropriate to speak of a person as "individuated," as might have been done in Jung's day, there are some generalizations that can be made about people who have enjoyed a productive Jungian analysis or have learned to integrate the unconscious by some other means, and I have included some quotable descriptions in Endpoints, Part III.

Jung said that in psychotherapy it seemed advisable that the doctor "should not have too fixed an aim." ("The Aims of Psychotherapy," CW 16, par. 81.) I think Wilfred Bion meant the same from the Freudian position when he recommended that therapists let go of all memories and desires when going into a therapy session. You can see from what has been said in previous chapters that it is risky to try to articulate the goal of individuation as it cannot be generalized, but there are some consistent advantages that we can expect to experience in the process.

In Jolande Jacobi's classical work she writes:

> Most people look unremittingly for "happiness," and it never occurs to them that happiness is not the goal of life set for them by the Creator. The true goal is a task that continues right up to life's evening, namely, the most complete and comprehensive development of personality. It is this which gives life an incomparable value that can never be lost: inner peace, and therefore the highest form of happiness. (Jacobi, *The Way of Individuation*, p. 17.)

Previously I said that individuation was not necessarily meant to make us happy. Neither could we be at peace if our individuation demands that we work in areas of outer conflict and turmoil. Working with the incurably sick, with refugees, with trauma, disastrous environmental problems, endangered species, poverty and hopeless social problems, fighting wars, fighting crooked politics and crime...are those who choose to enter these areas of struggle expected to know inner peace? And what of our passions? What happens to passion if we are imbued with inner peace? Such questions require more discussion.

To begin, let us consider this passage from Jeffrey Raff, in which Raff differentiates the latent from the manifest Self:

> If the manifest self is alive in the soul, we are able to meet every situation with the appropriate response. We are kind when kindness is appropriate and severe when severity is required. We are not afraid of our own dark side, nor are we dominated by it, but express it in a suitable manner; we see the creative spirit in the material world and enjoy material pleasures...we are unafraid to express all sides of our personality and repress none. Our willingness to be all that we are, and to embrace all of our parts, allows us to experience ourselves as whole beings. (Raff, *Jung and the Alchemical Imagination*, p. 15.)

This experience of being "whole," or fully ourselves, or the still point, is in itself a place of inner peace, no matter in what circumstances we find ourselves. In good times or in extreme adversity, there is a satisfaction that comes from being integrated and from simply being. A kind of contentment permeates being, even in the face of pain and sorrow. Even when faced with death, though the body may react with distress and signs of anxiety or sadness, the soul finds it bearable and can experience gratitude, a state of loving empathy, and union with all beings.

The connection between the ego and the Self is often imaged as a sacred marriage. When one experiences a continuity of connection as a usual state, we feel the bond becoming stronger and more accessible, as more and more one comes to feel united in love with other beings and with the divine in its ever-changing, myriad forms.

We call it the "process of individuation" because it *is* a process. The peace described here is not often found in the early part of the process. Although I have met little children who seemed to be wiser than most adults and more at peace in the face of pain as well as young people who were farther along in the process of inner peace than some adults ever get, it is generally true that peace is easier to come to in old age, when we have gratifying life experiences to look back on. For most people who reach old age, many desires have been met and satisfied. That being said, the process is not about age or getting what we want, but about connecting with the source of psychic energy. That is why most descriptions of individuation include the adjectives "vibrant," "lively," "open," "grateful," "intense," and the like.

It is essential to understand that it is a two-way process between the person we are and the source of psyche. There is a human ego and a source of larger consciousness. We can touch the source or Self without being individuated, and that can be wonderful or problematic.

When we touch the energy of the Self directly, we know it. The feelings are unmistakably strong. In its positive state it is described as feeling confident, centered, ecstatic, of being loved and being loving, a sense of inner partnership with a strong ground under our being. In its negative state it is described as utter hopelessness.

Being in the presence of the Self is an important aspect of individuation, but it is not in itself individuation. When my friend Sally felt so ecstatic that she ran through the streets naked, singing and laughing, we did not feel happy for her. We swiftly gathered her in our arms and

got her to a treatment center. If we had had a well-organized community response, as in some tribal cultures, or as Janet Dallett describes in
her book, *When the Spirits Come Back*, we might have seen Sally through
this psychotic episode without institutionalizing her. She was not just
in the presence of the Self; she was overwhelmed by it and had no ego
strength to channel her ecstasy appropriately. She was in a state of psychic inflation, which is always a danger to oneself and others.

A less extreme example is Jean, who considers herself beloved of
God. Jean's faith is her Self symbol, and so her conscious ego is united
with the Self most of the time, and she feels good. But she is not interested in individuating. She does not examine her choices, or question
the beliefs of her faith, nor does she express curiosity about her own
dark side—her inability to express doubt, her resentment, envy, mean-
spirited criticisms of people who are different—which she expresses in
unconscious ways. Jean's one-sided relationship with the Self is detect-
able by a lack of empathy; sooner or later one bumps up against Jean's
shadow, where no dialogue is possible.

When my friend Carl was overcome by the Self, he did not run
through the streets; he could not move or speak. He felt he was in hell,
paralyzed with fear, and he was a captive of the Self for months. He
also was inflated, but in a negative way, believing he was exception-
ally worthless, a damnable being. He had touched the dark, destructive
state of the Self.

In these cases the ego was not yet able to have a dialogue with the
Self, and imbalance or psychosis occurred. In another condition, when
we contact the Self through drugs, we may feel fine and powerful, or
bad and powerless. We may write about it or describe it, but we are not
engaging in ego-Self dialogue; we are possessed by the Self. Temporary
experiences of transformation come with unusual conditions—starva-
tion, fever, immersion in art and music, for example—but they do not
even contribute to individuation until they are subjected to the careful
process of inner dialogue and consistent conscious reflection. Jung described such temporary states of inflation as the ego being assimilated
by the Self.

When charismatic leaders are possessed by the Self, their omnipotent
feelings are contagious. Their followers will drink poison, blow themselves up, or fight wars in the thrall of the energy of the Self that comes
through the leader. But it is not the state achieved through individua-

tion, a state which comes after long work of engagement between ego and unconscious culminating in the serenity that comes with knowing one's limits.

The other extreme of the ego-Self connection, doing good work in strengthening the ego while denying the Self, is also not individuation. Good intentions and careful attention to outer life situations are not enough, for without the experience of discernment which comes from learning to work with the unconscious, we do not recognize the Self when it appears. If we do notice it, we see it as nothing but coincidence, or we reduce the energy of the Self to a biological or physical explanation.

My friend Martin can't imagine being out of control like Sally and Carl were (which doesn't mean he might not find himself there someday; he is also vulnerable to psychosis, as we all are to some degree). Martin has been a psychotherapist for years and is a staunch behaviorist. He does not remember dreams, does not believe in a soul, and finds the concept of the unconscious unsupportable. He works hard to learn his profession. He treats others well and respectfully and tries to maintain a healthy body. He helps his patients to create good relationships and work ethics, to overcome fears, and to find comfortable adjustments and happy lives. He may be trying to individuate, but he does not accept the basic premise, which is that his ego is not in control; therefore, he will not know transcendence through dialogue with the Self, unless fate chooses to force it upon him.

Should he ever become acquainted with the inner life of the soul, he may come to understand that "when the ego does Active Imagination and enters the world of the unconscious, it now feels as if it is going to meet its lover." (Raff, *Jung and the Alchemical Imagination*, p. 111.) Martin does not know that it is possible to contact the imaginal world while maintaining a stance in reality. He can submit his view of dreams and intuitions to doubt, but he can't submit his belief in materialistic philosophy to doubt. He cannot imagine a reality that might unite physical and psychical perceptions. Jung describes this attitude as the Self assimilated to the ego.

Now, what about passion? Is it still possible in the transformative state, when one is in love with the Self? Can there be a lover without when there is a lover within? Yes, unequivocally yes! Because the body is present, not repressed but very much alive, everything the body feels is present in individuation. Love of a partner is more complete and satisfying than ever. Yet, many earlier passions and desires arise and seem petty, not worth the time. Some are channeled into beyond-ego issues, and we find ourselves dedicated to world-wide problems and cosmic questions. Injustice, greed, and dishonesty of all kinds cause exquisite distress, but we do not respond with despair. Our outrage is registered and asks for action but does not demand unbridled release.

I will end this reading with a thought from Marie-Louise von Franz, as she speaks about fairy tales:

> Although the inner order refuses to be schematized, we can nevertheless obtain hints of that order by observing that all the different tales circumambulate one and the same content—the Self. (von Franz, *Interpretation of Fairy Tales*, p. 147)

In the wonder of the Self, no matter what fate determines, you always return to your center with awe, open and grateful.

> *I don't feel frightened by not knowing things, by being lost in the mysterious universe without having any purpose, which is the way it really is, as far as I can tell, possibly. It doesn't frighten me.*
>
> – Richard Feynman
> quoted in Reagan, *The Hand of God*

Part III

Lagniappe

I

A Question of Principle

Part I began with that attitude of inquiry from an alchemist, and Part II ended with similar thoughts from a prominent physicist, Richard Feynman.

Although many of us do not know of any purpose we might have in the universe and do not find that thought frightening, we are free to conjecture, imagine, and believe for the pure joy of imagining.

Some who have considered the possibility of finding meaning in the universe conclude that they must say their "ironic goodnight to sacred order." (Philip Rieff, quoted in Gundry, *Beyond Psyche: Symbol and Transcendence in C.G. Jung*, p. 18.) Doubters such as Rieff, and Richard Dawkins present impressive arguments against meaning.

Others think that order is built into the human brain, and not "out there." "Universal themes of religion are not learned. They merge as accidental by-products of our mental systems. They are part of human nature," says Yale research psychologist Paul Bloom. (Bloom, "Is God an Accident?" p. 4.)

Neither epistemology nor scientific research can be exempt from the charges of subjectivity, its confines, limits, and biases. If there is no point outside of the human condition from which to view reality, is there any answer to nihilism? Is there such a thing as truth? Yes, say many who believe that continued conversation between disciplines advances understanding, even without a permanent background of "reality" to steady us. We do not need to subscribe to a naïve view of "truth" in order to make distinctions between degrees of truth. Every language-game, discipline, and philosophy, including those which support nihilism or atheism, holds to a standard of truth and a principle of order to communicate its principles.

The methods of the hard-sciences are not often useful for psychological inquiry. Efforts are being made to find appropriate ways of researching the subtleties in the humanities. Post-enlightenment hermeneutics allows an appreciation of scholarly research into art, history, politics, psychology, and the like, to convey truths to the degree that they contribute relevance to our lives. A recent discussion of these issues can be found in Mark Gundry's answer to the "hermeneutics of suspicion." (Gundry, *Beyond Psyche*.)

Jung never answered the question of whether he believed in a divine presence. He did once say in an interview, when asked if he believed, "I do not believe, I know." ("Face to Face: Professor Jung," British Broadcasting Corporation, 1959.) That has been subjected to mixed interpretations. One interpretation notes that he could have been speaking as an empiricist who knew through observation of the archetypal world, or as a Gnostic knows by examining his inner world, or knowing metaphorically, always leaving ambiguity in his responses, while he calculatedly did not admit to belief.

Late in life Jung wrote, "There is nothing I am quite sure about. I have no definite convictions—not about anything, really." (Jung, *Memories, Dreams, Reflections*, p. 358.) Ambiguity about aspects of the psyche that span the territory of the psychological and mystical is not uncommon, as Sanford Drob notes in describing his extensive research of the Kabbalah and its relationship to Analytical Psychology.

> Jung should be applauded for his intuitive recognition that only an ambiguous and paradoxical language can express certain matters regarding the psyche that cannot be expressed in either/or, linear form...the kabbalists and Hassidim (as do mystics of many traditions) refuse to make sharp distinctions between the outer and inner, the macrocosm and microcosm, the transcendent and the immanent, and the theological and the psychological, holding that such distinctions sever a primal unity and plunge one hopelessly into a (practically necessary, but) illusory world of dichotomous thinking and experience. (Drob, "Jung's Kabbalistic Visions," p. 49.)

John Dourley has noted that Jung's later writings leave no doubt of his non-dualist thought, compatible with Eastern religions. That is, Jung understands, as do the mystics, that the ego has access to humanity's native divinity in the depths of the unconscious. Such access to numinous experiences is both individual and universal. (Dourley, "Response to Barbara Stephens," pp. 479-492.)

Quite early in his career (1916), Jung wrote privately for his friends a kind of poem, in the style of ancient alchemists, which describes a view of the construction of the order of the entire cosmos. It can be thought of as a fantasy of a spiritual Self beyond the human level of being. These excerpts are from sermons one and three:

> The Nothing or fullness, is called by us the Pleroma. In it thinking and being cease, because the eternal is without qualities...
>
> If the Pleroma were capable of having a being, Abraxas would be its manifestation.
>
> Although he is activity itself, he is not a particular result but result in general.
>
> He is active non-reality because he has no definite result.
>
> He is still a created being inasmuch as he is differentiated from the Pleroma.
>
> For he is power, endurance, change.
>
> Man sees the summum bonum of the sun and also the infinum malum of the devil,
>
> but Abraxas he does not see, for he is indefinable life itself,
>
> which is the mother of good and evil alike.

This version is published in Hoeller. (Hoeller, *The Gnostic Jung and the Seven Sermons to the Dead*.) "Seven Sermons to the Dead" is also found as an appendix in Jung's autobiography, *Memories, Dreams, Reflections*.

2

Avoiding Recipes, Accepting Responsibility

As a therapist I continually witness evolution of consciousness in individual lives. I would like to believe that this shows that human consciousness not only can, but is, evolving, and that we can look forward to becoming a more intelligent, humane, and tolerant species. But it does not necessarily follow. Anthropologists have not agreed on whether substantial changes have evolved in the innate capacity for thought of human beings through the ages. "Emerging" and "unfolding," without putting a value of "getting better" on our development, describes more of what contemporary thinkers can agree to. We are suspicious about goals, teleologies, and anything smacking of hierarchical progress. Jungian thought tends toward being teleological, even though Jung was nondogmatic about using the term "teleology." (Nagy, *Philosophical Issues in the Psychology of C.G. Jung*, p. 263.)

> All we can say is that things happen as if there were a fixed final aim. In psychology one ought to be wary of believing absolutely in causality as of an absolute belief in teleology. ("The Relations Between the Ego and the Unconscious," CW 7, par. 501.)

• • •

In *Science of the Soul*, Edinger employed the image of three dimensions in reference to the therapist as medical person, philosopher, and priest. I find the image of three dimensions a convenient system of organizing approaches to psychological material. This three-dimensional approach allows space for a positivistic psychology, a humanistic and phenomenological psychology, and a spiritual psychology. The psychiatrist and philosopher, Maurice Nicoll, a colleague of Jung and student of philosopher Gurdjieff, used this concept of three dimensions to describe levels of psychic depth. These divisions also correspond to Jung's three stages of coniunctio in the alchemical individuation process, explicated in Part II, Chapter 9, as follows: 1) Unio Mentalis; 2) Re-union of body, soul, and spirit; and 3) Unus Mundus.

The collective unconscious is sometimes called the "objective psyche." It is at the heart of Jung's work to recognize that we feel we are in charge of our minds and souls, but our minds and souls are also beyond us; they contain contents that we do not control, that feel as if they come from outside, so they are "the objects" of our interest and attention. Edward Edinger says that the objective psyche sees you as its object, which gives meaning to the well-known symbol of the "Eye of God," which sees us. The "Eye of God" is an example of an archetypal image which can be positive or negative, depending on the interpretation given it by the person receiving the image. One person feels the seeing god to be benevolently watching over them; another feels persecuted by the continual, suspicious spy in the sky.

I was interested to see that this idea that we are not just subjects of thought, but objects of thought, has reached popular culture and public acceptance, as noted in James Wood's piece in *The New Yorker*, "The Unforgotten." Wood wrote:

> ...a good portion of reality consists of what we freely imagine; and then, less happily perhaps, we discover that that reality has imagined us—that we are the vassals of our imaginings, not their emperors or archdukes. (Wood, "The Unforgotten," p. 83.)

To begin studying Jung, it is helpful to know that he drew a diagram to illustrate the structure of the unconscious. As described by C. Michael Smith: The lowest level he called the "central fire," a cosmic source of energy that penetrates all the other layers. Next was the layer of animal ancestry, then the layer of primeval ancestry, and above this a layer representing the psychical deposits and structures of large cultural groups, all interconnected. These comprise the deep layers of archetypal images which form the patterns of human behavior. The higher layers were more specific to the culture and the individual. They included the layer of nation, then the layer of family, and finally the layer of the individual. In special states of consciousness the archaic layers, which are normally operating unconsciously, can be activated. The imagery produced usually is felt to be numinous and compelling. (Smith, *Jung and Shamanism in Dialogue*, p. 105.)

Aspects of this kind of layered diagram can be detected in designs, photography, alchemical texts, and art objects throughout the world. It is stimulating to play with such images on one's own, to find ways of depicting the inner life as one experiences it, as a form of active imagination and individuation. The concept of a collective unconscious that can potentially be identified by physiological research has its supporters in psychobiology as well as its skeptics and detractors. It is a developing concept in Analytical Psychology.

3

Reality of the Psyche

Later in Jung's essay on philosophy cited in Part I, Chapter 3, he writes, "Naturally I am familiar with Leibnitz, C.G. Carus, and von Hartmann, but I never knew till now that my psychology is 'Romantic.'" ("Foreword to Mehlich, 'Fichte's Psychology and Its Relation to the Present,'" CW 18, par. 1730 and 1732.)

Claire Douglas sees in Jung a war between Positivism and Romanticism, but one that enabled him to use science to legitimately justify the study of the irrational. (Young-Eisendrath and Dawson, eds., *The Cambridge Companion to Jung*, p. 20.)

Marilyn Nagy's research into Jung's influences led her to conclude that he was a "metaphysical idealist." But I don't think that label does justice to his grounding in life's realities: his experience in hospitals, clinics, and consulting rooms; his skeptical observation of occult practitioners; his concerned listening to psychotics and hearing their explanations for their beliefs; his insistence that active imagination include the ego's point of view; his attempts to work with Wolfgang Pauli on physical theories of energy; his collecting of data on dreams, typology, and universal symbols; his insistence on the unity of mind and bodily emotions, not just in the individual but in his theory of archetypes; his use of physical methods and artistic activities; and his very physical approach to life.

Jung's mind wandered and wondered into philosophical territory with alacrity, and his curiosity was not tethered to the tangible world. He was exquisitely sensitive to spiritual questions and open to imaginal stratospheres. But no one who reads him thoroughly could stamp Jung with finality as an idealist. He was undeniably a ponderer of all and an observer of all. Nagy herself admits that in her clinical work she maintains a relationship with Jung's attitude that does not strictly match her philosophical judgment.

It was very important to Jung and Freud to have the respect of their scientifically oriented professional communities. Since the great scientific revolution was so impressive, we have a tendency to think of science as infallible. Its proofs often seem unquestionable. It is important to distinguish science, a human endeavor, from scientism, an inordinate idealization of science that regards science as faultless, in the same manner as a fundamentalist regards his religion. Logical positivism was a philosophical movement in the early twentieth century which nurtured this idealization. It aimed to rid philosophy of metaphysics and to insure that everything offered had been verified beyond question.

But depth psychology never completely shed the aura of metaphysics. Curtis D. Smith discusses the contradiction between Jung's description of himself as an objective empiricist and his statements about the ultimate nature and purpose of human existence in his book, *Jung's Quest for Wholeness: A Religious and Historical Perspective*.

Karl Popper contributed to the process of scientific and philosophical verification by showing that a meaningful hypothesis must be falsifiable. There is no way to test Jung's hypothesis of the collective psyche. No matter how much we might find an idea foolish or believable, ideas are *neither* scientifically false nor true unless they can be tested and disproved, according to Popper.

Scientists finally admitted that they themselves could not be totally objective and had to look at themselves more realistically. Scientists like Michael Polanyi opposed positivism and thought that scientists were naturally influenced by their beliefs and biases and needed to be permitted to work in a free environment, not under any fixed system or government. He influenced philosopher Paul Feyerabend, who insisted that scientists were not gods but humans subject to the same problems as humans in any other business—problems that colored their objectivity, such as envy, exaggeration, and opportunism. He represented the coming of an attitude of relativism and proposed that we accept whatever works at a particular moment to advance our knowledge.

Many scientists complain that pressure to get academic tenure biases ideas and quashes creativity. In short, innovation and unconventionality by writers, politicians, scientists, and artists, and the capacity to think outside the popular views, is not rewarded in our current titanic monetary systems.

The rampant greed in society moved hand-in-hand with nihilism. Though nihilism still is palpable, there is some evidence of a shift toward appreciation of mystery. John Adams, composer of the contemporary opera "Dr. Atomic," wrote about his journey from minimalism to deeply appreciating music that reflected caring (for example, Wagner's caring to make the intensity of his emotions palpable to the listener). Adams describes Wagner's "sense of ravishment... As a governing aesthetic, minimalism would rapidly exhaust itself. Like cubism in painting, it was a radical idea, but its reductive worldview would soon leave its practitioners caught in an excessive bind. Picasso saw the pregnant possibility of cubism, but he also realized that it must eventually be absorbed into a larger, more embracing language." (Adams, "Sonic Youth," p. 37.)

David Foster Wallace, a popular young author interviewed by Terry Gross on National Public Radio in the U.S.A., had a similar observation. He said that he and his associates had been terrified of being perceived as naïve or gullible and therefore felt they had to be slick and clever to gain money, fame, or sex. But, said Wallace, that attitude became tiresome. The twenty-first century has witnessed irony and satire running out of steam and being replaced by a longing for genuine emotion. (Wallace killed himself in 2007, not long after giving that interview.)

For a discussion of how deconstruction may lead to a hunger for mystery, see David Tacey's discussion in *The Idea of the Numinous*. Tacey considers the example of Jacques Derrida, the father of philosophic deconstruction, who spent the last fifteen years of life concerned with religion, remembering his orthodox Jewish youth spent in sincere prayer. Tacey feels Derrida tried to recover what he had lost as a clever, cynical intellectual:

> One unexpected impact of post-modernism has been the restoration of the pivotal role of imagination, play and the symbolic mode in life, art and culture... One of Derrida's leading colleagues, Gianni Vattimo, has made this recent comment that should awaken Jungians from their resistance to the postmodern as an authentic experiment in consciousness: today continental philosophers speak increasingly, and without providing explicit justification, about angels, redemption, and various mythological figures... the "ephemeral" productions of the imaginal realm, the "inconsequential" works of myth and dream, the rela-

tive "trivia" of metaphor and fantasy, are all we have left after the collapse of established systems of meaning. (Tacey, letter posted on the online discussion forum, The International Association for Jungian Studies, September, 2008, http://www.jungianstudies.org.)

Tacey says that Derrida called "spirit" by various names, such as "gift," "messianic," and "the impossible." (Casement and Tacey, *The Idea of the Numinous*, p. 63.)

Contemporary physicist Lee Smolin wrote:

We, who can dream of infinite time and space, of the infinitely beautiful and the infinitely good, find ourselves embedded in several worlds: the physical world, the social world, the imaginative world, and the spiritual world... It's a condition of being human that we have long sought to discover crafts that give us power over these diverse worlds. These crafts are now called science, politics, art and religion. Now, as in our earliest days, they give us power over our lives and form the basis of our hopes. Whatever they have been called, there has never been a human society without science, politics, art and religion. In caves whose walls are adorned with the paintings of ancient hunters, we have found bones and rocks with patterns showing that people were counting something in groups of fourteen, twenty-eight or twenty-nine. (Smolin, *The Trouble with Physics*, p. 298.)

Whether these ancient number systems were observations of the phases of the moon, menstrual cycles, or something else, it tells us that 20,000 years ago people were using mathematics to organize their experience of nature. Smolin reminds us that *every* conclusion is based on incomplete evidence. Science moves forward only when scientists are open-minded.

4

A Philosophical Moment

To give depth psychology a historical and cultural perspective, I recommend Henri Ellenberger's *The Discovery of the Unconscious*. There the roots of psychology are traced back through ancient history. Also see Claire Douglas, "The Historical Context of Analytical Psychology" in *The Cambridge Companion to Jung*, pp. 17-34.)

Ellenberger discusses Anaximander's sixth century intuition: he saw a boundless universe, and he anticipated Darwin's theory of evolution. These are examples of ideas that come not from scientific observation, but from a depth of mind compatible with the notion of the collective unconscious. (Ellenberger, *The Discovery of the Unconscious*, p. 734; p. 229.) In Ellenberger we grasp the full influence of Romanticism on psychoanalysis. An essential feature of Romanticism is the belief in the unity of spirit and matter.

The attempt to demonstrate unity of matter and spirit was the goal of alchemy, as Jung showed, and it excites the imagination today. Robert Grinnell says:

> Today we are entering what might be called a new animism...we have only the most rudimentary ideas of the way in which energy, and especially psychic energy, can manifest itself. This animism is like the discovery of a world... "Matter" is again beginning to show qualities that in ancient times were attributed to divinity... If such should prove the case, then we are assisting in the creation of a new myth... But this process belongs primarily to the procession of the aeons and only secondarily to the individuals who are its carriers. (Grinnell, *Alchemy in a Modern Woman*, p. 164.)

The sense of a vast and unified cosmos was present in the collective consciousness from earliest history. Giordano Bruno, a Dominican monk, was burned at the stake because he intuited that the cosmos consisted of many heliocentric universes, and that God resided in the stuff of the unified world, a world consisting of atomic particles filled with the love of God. Though the Inquisition found him wrong, science has proved him right. Imagine the electrified, magnetized, primordial energy of the basic particle and its potential for creation and utter destruction as the literal presence of divine love!

Jung's long-term collaboration with the Nobel prize-winning physicist Pauli rested on their mutual belief that the oneness of psyche and matter would be demonstrated someday. They sought that unity in the phenomenon of synchronicity. After years of collaborative exploring of the concept of synchronicity, they came to believe that it made possible a unitary worldview in which science and philosophy came together to revise the theory of the relationship of mind and matter. (Meier, *Atom and Archetype*.)

Yet we must observe caution, philosopher Ken Wilbur points out, because, though science and spirituality are both necessary for an integral approach to reality, neither can be reduced to nor derived from the other. He quotes Max Planck on the reality of the external world:

> [Theoretical physics] may, to some extent, satisfy the metaphysical hunger which religion does not seem capable of satisfying nowadays. But this would be entirely by stimulating the religious reaction indirectly. Science as such can never really take the place of religion. (Wilbur, *Quantum Questions*, p. 164.)

Throughout these chapters I have referred to different personality types. For a depth understanding of personality types, see Jung's CW 6, particularly the section on the Apollonian and the Dionysian. Nietzsche popularized this contrast between two gods of ancient Greece, whose contradictory natures could illustrate certain patterns in all areas of human activity. Jung's colleague, anthropologist Karl Kerényi, presents a more scholarly and sober approach in his book *Dionysos: Archetypal Image of Indestructible Life*, which serves to balance the poetic/erratic Nietzschean view of Dionysus as intoxicator. (Kerényi, *Dionysos*.)

Other images of typological differences are illustrative. Susan Rowland, in critiquing Jung as a writer (Rowland, *Jung as a Writer*), discusses the centripetal/centrifugal organizing principles. Lucy Huskinson (Huskinson, *Dreaming the Myth Onwards*) discusses the polarities in terms of integrative and pluralistic tendencies. Jungian psychoanalyst John Beebe, an authority on typology, has extensively researched the relationship between typology, ethics, and integrity. (Burleson and Beebe, *Pathways to Integrity: Ethics and Psychological Types*.) For a discussion of the way typology influences our choice of spiritual expression, see *Psyche and the Sacred*, by Lionel Corbett.

5

Defining Psyche, Soul, Mind, and Spirit

Explanations of the terms defined in this chapter are also found in Samuels (*A Critical Dictionary of Jungian Analysis*), Sharp (*Jung Lexicon: A Primer of Terms and Concepts*), and Corbett (*Psyche and the Sacred: Spirituality Beyond Religion*). They all provide rich and comprehensive discussions of soul and spirit.

Comparing archeology and neurology, Lewis-Williams and Pearce conclude that religion and cosmology are embedded in our neurology, as perceptions of invisible realms derive from electro-chemical functions of the brain. Their research convinced them that, from the beginning of time, humankind has been wired to accept the reality of the supernatural. (Lewis-Williams and Pearce, *Inside the Neolithic Mind: Consciousness, Cosmos and the Realm of the Gods.*)

James Hillman's classic essay, "Peaks and Vales: The Soul-Spirit Distinction as Basis for Differences between Psychotherapy and Spiritual Discipline," describes soul and spirit in a way that gives depth and honor to the terms. (Hillman, *Puer Papers.*) Hillman writes, "The mind never stops oozing and spurting the sap and juice of fantasy, and then congealing this play into paranoid monuments of eternal truth." (Hillman, "Peaks and Vales," in *Puer Papers*, p. 126.)

About the archetype Anima/Animus: In Part II, chapter 12, gender is a focus, but for the time being I would point out that contemporary Jungians see Anima/Animus present in everyone in varying degrees on a conscious level, thanks to the groundwork laid by Jung and the popularization of his "inner feminine and masculine" concept. Contrary to the classical expectation, people often enter analysis with motives provoked by Anima/Animus issues, rather than Shadow issues. These Anima/Animus concerns relate to questions of relationship, and ultimately to connection with the Self; they seem to guide us to deep experiences of soul, regardless of the gender of the archetypal image.

In their book, *A General Theory of Love*, psychiatrists Lewis, Amini, and Lannon suggest that we form attractions to people with familiar emotional (limbic area) brain rhythms. They say, "A relationship that strays from one's prototype is limbically equivalent to isolation.... Most people will choose misery with a partner their limbic brain recognizes over the stagnant pleasure of a 'nice' relationship with someone their attachment mechanisms cannot detect." (Lewis, et al., *A General Theory of Love*, p. 161.) Limbic attractors formed in childhood are the strongest, which explains why we gravitate to people who remind us of early relationships. Therapy can help to stop this self-perpetuating drive to unsatisfying relationships by retraining limbic relatedness through relationship with the therapist. However, although the neocortex quickly learns cognitive facts, the limbic brain requires lots of repetition to be reprogrammed, a primary reason why long-term therapy cannot be replaced by a quick fix.

The authors say, "What Richard Selzer, M.D., once wrote of surgery is as true of therapy: only human love keeps this from being the act of two madmen." (Lewis, et al., *A General Theory of Love*, p. 190.) Two beings sitting alone together for hours, exploring the inner experiences of one while the other tracks his/her responses to the material...are they mad? Therapy as the act of two madmen, sustained by love...what an image!

6

Self

Jung maintained that the Self could not be defined or known through the intellect, but only through experiencing it, a view consistent with that of the Buddha, the skeptic philosopher David Hume, Friedrich Nietzsche, and others. These are some summaries of Jung's philosophical influences listed in the bibliography:

> C.G. Jung, "The Self," CW 9ii, Chapter IV.
>
> C.G. Jung, "Psychological Types," CW 6, especially Chapters I, II, III.
>
> Henri Ellenberger, *The Discovery of the Unconscious*, especially Chapter 9, and discussions of Immanuel Kant, Friedrich Hegel, Ignaz Troxler, Rudolf Steiner, and others.
>
> Andrew Samuels, *Jung and the Post-Jungians*, especially Chapter 4.
>
> Edward Edinger, *The Creation of Consciousness*.
>
> Sean Kelly, *Individuation and the Absolute: Hegel, Jung and the Path Toward Wholeness*.
>
> Stephen A. Hoeller, *The Gnostic Jung and the Seven Sermons to the Dead*.
>
> Lucy Huskinson, *Nietzsche and Jung: The Whole Self in the Union of Opposites*.

Whether Jung was aware of it or not, the worldview of Giovanni Battista Vico, seventeenth century historian, held to a view of history that anticipated Jung's attraction to the quaternary as a symbol of the Self. Vico, an important influence on James Joyce, proposed a historical pattern as a progression of four recurring eras: the theocratic (era of gods); the aristocratic (era of heroes); the democratic (era of men); and then the dissolution of the society as it reverted to another theocratic era on a more advanced plane. (See Verene, "Coincidence, historical repetition, and self-knowledge: Jung, Vico, and Joyce.")

In an essay, "'Divinity expresses the Self...' An Investigation," Murray Stein explores the complex relation of the Self to the transcendent, to make the case that Jung's psychology represents a post-Enlightenment, post-secular, post-humanistic vision of the human as a material/spiritual being:

> Expressed in the psyche as an archetype, the self is the source and point of origin of all human elaborated mythologies and theologies, even if it is not a complete or accurate description of the "unfathomable Being" itself. (Stein, "Individuation: Inner Work," p. 314.)

Jung's conflict with Christianity, with which he wrestled all his life and which has been explored so well by Stein, John Dourley, Ann Lammers, David Tacey, and others, was largely over his insistence that the Self contained all opposites and produced images of good and evil.

The problem of evil and the dark side of the Self that Jung and theologian Victor White struggled with continues to stir philosophers, psychologists, and theologians. For example, Lucy Huskinson analyzes Emmanuel Levinas's idea of Other-and-Same as it relates to Jung's Self. (Huskinson, *The Self as Violent Other*, p. 444.)

Mary Watkins, representative of the mercurial approach to personality, points out that "development" exists only as a result of our theories, with the exception of physiological development. Psychological faculties do not assume hierarchical priorities, and imagination is an innate factor which is expressed in multiplicities of no apparent order.

Jungian psychoanalyst James Hillman's work has been dedicated to relativizing what he perceives as a dominating focus on ego and Self, resulting in the diminishment and lack of attention to other essential aspects of psyche, the archetypes, and the imagination. As a result of that line of thought, the movement called "Archetypal Psychology" (and now often referred to as "Archetypal Psychologies") arose and was identified by Samuels. (Samuels, *Jung and the Post-Jungians*.) Jungian psychoanalyst Michael Vannoy Adams describes the purpose of Archetypal Psychology to be animation—the animation of the ego into soul. (Young-Eisendrath and Dawson, eds., *The Cambridge Companion to Jung*, p. 113.) Adams said in a tribute to Hillman that in order to re-vision psychology, Hillman had to repudiate the Self as the "concept of concepts." This was a vital step in bringing to the forefront of our thought the importance of the particular archetypal image, and the non-judgmental acceptance of all the vagaries, diversities, and pluralities of psyche's movement.

Hillman rightly saw that with too much focus on the archetype of the Self we were in danger of losing touch with the human element, with the reality of death and suffering, and with the diversity of the larger culture. We could become advocates of a constricting monotheistic approach, more arbiters of good taste and right behavior than compassionate psychologists for real people in a many-faceted and constantly changing world. Hillman became annoyed with a provincial tendency in Zurich for analysts to be seen as almighty priests of the true god. Archetypal Psychology helps to balance any veering toward fundamentalism in the field.

My intention is to present a case for the primary place of Self in the individuation process without damaging or denigrating the wisdom of every possible divine image and without seeming moralistic. I am advocating certain values, even as I try to allow space for the values of others. I hope that every reader will embrace the idea of knowing themselves, their conscious mind and its unconscious counterpart.

Robert Grinnell writes of the "shedding of the compulsive character—the horoscope imprinted on each person at his birth..." We can free ourselves from the mind-set behind the belief that "neurotic symptoms are... unalterable hereditary genetic facts which it is useless to resist." (Grinnell, *Alchemy in a Modern Woman*, p. 93) This is a challenging statement. We are in danger of succumbing to this reductive thinking because of several trends: the exciting discoveries of genetics, remarkable drugs to treat psychological problems, and new refinements in neuroscience making possible the linking of behavior to brain function. Contrary to that leaning toward biological determinism, neuroscience can support the fact that what were once thought to be inflexible brain processes are now seen as being alterable through new learning and new experiences. For more about this, see the publications of Allan Schore, Antonio Damasio, Gerard Edelman, and others. This topic is impelling an abundance of research, more than space allows here.

The temptation to give up on psychological change in the face of evidence of biological determinism is strongly encouraged in our culture. That seduction is answered in this opinion from Eric Kandel, Nobel prize-winner in physiology, as quoted by Ernest Rossi: "The regulation of gene expression by social factors makes all bodily functions, including all functions of the brain, susceptible to social influences." (Rossi, "Creativity and the Notion of the Numinosum," p. 325.)

An essay by reporter Lawrence Wright noted a shift in American attitudes in the 1990s that reflected both doubt that government can improve peoples' lives and skepticism regarding the possibility of personal transformations. This shift could be traced in the retreat from social activism, the cuts in welfare and job-training programs, and cuts in tax support for public education as research into behavioral genetics affected social policy. The shift in attitude followed an emphasis on genetic influence over environmental influences.

The jury is out about whether freedom depends more on genetics or experience, but meanwhile, in order to function responsibly, we assume we have some degree of freedom of choice over our behavior. Here I am arguing that it is not just possible, but essential that we exercise that choice and become the person we can and want to be. It would be prudent to lean toward the side of freedom in constructing social programs to give the best possible chance of helping all people make healthy choices in their lives. Despite the cultural trend toward determinism, if you can read this, personal transformation is possible for you.

Transformation in Jungian terms means becoming your true self. Psychoanalyst Jeffrey Raff describes the process of psychological transformation and its effect on the Self:

> Every time the ego contacts an image from the unconscious and engages it in meaningful dialogue, it can trigger the transcendent function. Every time it does so, no matter how small the issue involved may seem, it has strengthened and transformed the self. (Raff, *Jung and the Alchemical Imagination*, p. 22.)

Most of us can entertain the idea of flexibility and plasticity of the body and psyche. However, the idea that man could have an effect on God, which was the subject of *Answer to Job*, put Jung on the hot seat with theologians, particularly Martin Buber and Victor White. Jung's dialogues with these men and other theologians can be read in the collection of Jung's letters. Jung's claim that "Whoever knows God has an effect on Him" is easier to swallow when we look at the Self purely from the psychological dimension, in which God is an image in the psyche. But for those who conceive of God as a power beyond the human psyche, it seems highly arrogant for a human being to presume that he can "raise God's consciousness."

In the Swiss Reformed Christian tradition of Jung's father, the notion of the soul's direct and immediate relationship to God was accepted, and the idea of having a god who might be persuaded did not seem as farfetched as it did to those who perceived a god beyond human interaction. Jung's emotional response to the story of Job can be understood as a stepping outside of the ordinary submissiveness to whatever terrible things God allows to happen. Jung saw Job as representing a consciousness beyond mere passivity, a consciousness advanced enough to question the divine nature that was described by the anthropomorphic God-image of the time. In Jung's view, Job's movement away from passivity and into evaluating and questioning marked an important leap in the history of man's relationship to God. The movement wove together an intellectual picture of God with an emotional reaction from his creature, which Jung saw as an affirmation of the individuation process in the human psyche.

Edward Edinger, Erich Neumann, and others have spoken to the idea of contributing to the consciousness of the divine: for example, Janet Dallett (*The Not-yet Transformed God*); Nikos Kazantzakis (*The Saviors of God*); and Harold S. Kushner (*When Bad Things Happen to Good People*).

But more heretical to theologians was the notion that the divinity contained evil as well as good, a belief that Jung found necessary to explain the notion of the Self's completion. Jung felt misunderstood by Martin Buber. With Victor White, though, he had a respectful disagreement about the Thomistic belief in *privatio boni*, the belief that there is only good in God, and evil is not a quality but is the absence of good. Their argument about this could never be resolved. That is the subject of Ann Lammers's book, *In God's Shadow: The Collaboration of Victor White and C.G. Jung.*

7

A Brief History of Individuation

It seems that an entirely new conversation about individuation is happening in post-Jungian thought, and here we will try to sort out some of the issues. James Hillman refers to "that old conundrum of individuation on the one hand, collectivity on the other." (Hillman, *The Myth of Analysis*, p. 295.) Like the individuation process, we may not reach perfect clarification of the conundrum here; rather, we will enjoy the process.

Of the contemporary research into the relationship of consciousness to matter, Douglas Hofstadter has described in popular works the confusing loops of logic that beset our attempts to find identity.

> A creature that thinks knows next to nothing of the substrate allowing its thinking to happen, but nevertheless it knows all about its symbolic interpretation of the world, and knows very intimately something it calls "I." (Hofstadter, *I Am a Strange Loop*, p. 173.)

Someone who has attempted to explore those loops is Gerard Edelman. In *A Universe of Consciousness: How Matter Becomes Imagination*, Edelman and Giulio Tononi describe their brain research, which in my opinion supports Jung's complex theory. The observation of neuronal networks which form a recurrent pattern of experience and behavior could describe the physiology of a complex as Jung conceived it psychologically. They also show that each person has a unique "conscious footprint," in support of our theme of individuality. (Edelman, *A Universe of Consciousness: How Matter Becomes Imagination*.)

While the microscopic scale is not immediately applicable to a clinician, it is still inspiring to read Roger Penrose's investigations into the action of neurons from a theory of quantum mechanics, as he attempts to enter the mind/body mystery from the standpoint of quantum physics. His discussion of computer-like particles at the synapses, and, like

Hofstadter (*Gödel, Escher, Bach*), his use of the mathematical genius of Kurt Gödel, may not be completely clear to a non-mathematician, but we can appreciate the general quality of his search to resolve the Platonic split between the world of forms and the world of matter. (Penrose, *The Large, the Small, the Human Mind*.)

Research that is easily accessible is that of neuroscientist Allan Schore in his studies of infant/mother non-verbal interaction that can only be followed through magnetic resonance imaging (MRI). Neuroscientists of his ilk have demonstrated what depth psychologists have always intuited: good mothering is essential to healthy physical and mental functioning, not only in childhood, but in a person's vulnerability to post-traumatic stress and immunological disorders throughout life. (Schore, "The Effect of Early Relational Trauma on Right Brain Development, Affect Regulation, and Infant Mental Health.")

Not only does the infant's brain develop neural pathways that are modeled by the mother's brain, but the infant's heart responds to electrical, hormonal, neural, and sound patterns of the mother's heart, in utero, and during the post-birth bonding period through a process called "entrainment."

According to the Institute of HeartMath, research shows that electromagnetic frequencies of the brain and the heart can be trained to be in sync by a learning experience which reduces stress and allows new paths of response to open. When brain and heart frequencies entrain, they create synchronous wave patterns between mother and infant during breast feeding and close body contact. (Additional information available online at Institute of HeartMath (www.heartmath.org) or at 14700 West Park Avenue, Boulder Creek, CA 95006.)

Antonio Damasio shows that consciousness cannot be examined without including emotional data. He, P.M. Churchland, and many others continue the journey into the relationship between grey matter and abstract thought. Their investigations emphasize the complicated networks of information that surround the mystery of consciousness. Damasio warns about oversimplifying and overgeneralizing the effects of drugs on the psyche. For example, the findings at this stage of knowledge about the effects of serotonin on the hormonal system, though popular, are neither clear nor consistent. He underlines the complexity of the mind/body relationship:

On a practical note: The solution to the problem of social violence will not come from addressing only social factors and ignoring neurochemical correlates; nor will it come from blaming one neurochemical correlate alone. Considerations of BOTH social and neurochemical factors is required, in appropriate measure. (Damasio, *Descartes' Error*, p. 78.)

8

Two Ways of Individuating

Although some people can learn to integrate unconscious material naturally, more often the help of another experienced person is needed, especially in the case of extreme discomfort caused by psychological problems. Analysis is a long process, and until recently its benefits were not objectively established. As psychological research becomes more sophisticated, the value of long-term therapies, like psychoanalysis, is being confirmed. Some recent studies of Effectiveness of Long-term Psychodynamic Psychotherapy versus Short-term, Evidence-Based Therapy and Cognitive Behavioral Therapy include:

> "The Fall and Rise of Expertise," Roger Brooke, Ph.D., in *Bulletin of American Academy of Clinical Psychology*, Fall 05/ Winter 06, 10, 1, 8-10.

> "Effectiveness of LTPP: A Meta-analysis," Falk Leichsenring and Sven Rabung, *Journal of the American Medical Association*, 2008, 300:1551-1565.

> "Psychodynamic Psychotherapy and Research Evidence: Bambi Survives Godzilla?" Richard Glass, *Journal of the American Medical Association*, 2008, 300:1587-1589.

Scientific American published a review of critics and supporters of psychoanalysis in December, 1996, "Why Freud Isn't Dead," by John Horgan. The results of many studies of drugs and psychotherapy concluded that psychological interventions are at least as effective as medication in treating depression, even if severe. Another study showed that drugs produced significantly better outcomes in only a third of patients, but also that the effects of medication wane after a while and patients relapse. (Horgan, "Why Freud Isn't Dead," p. 110.)

Also, the 1995 *Consumer Reports'* survey of 4000 readers was reviewed: most reported that they had been helped by psychotherapy, and that the longer they remained in therapy, the more they felt they had improved. Those who received psychotherapy alone reported doing as well as those who were treated with a combination of psychotherapy and anti-depressants. Although obsessive-compulsive disorder was not specifically described in the studies, Martin Seligman, who was president of the American Psychological Association at the time as well as an authority on efficacy research, stated that, except for lithium for bipolar disorder and tranquilizers for schizophrenia, there is no evidence that medications are superior to talk therapies for more common disorders like depression and obsessive-compulsive disorder. (Horgan, "Why Freud Isn't Dead," p. 110.)

In observing reflective individuation, Murray Stein describes a two-phase movement. In the analytic phase, the attachments to, and unconscious identity with, certain inner structures (e.g., persona, anima-animus, childish theologies, the need to belong to some collectives — all that blocks and contaminates the unique personality) must be loosened through reflection and analysis. In the synthetic phase, we explore the deep, universal psychic structures that unconsciously influence us, physically and spiritually.

Because our spiritual needs touch upon such deep unconscious levels of the psyche, they awaken anxiety in many of us and create strong reactions in the public arena. The ability to resonate to spiritual impulses and ideas can be evoked but not taught. Stein points out that Jung's gift of sensibility to the spiritual dimension was extraordinary. (Stein, *The Principle of Individuation.*)

Attempts to identify stages of moral growth (Lawrence Kohlberg, Carol Gilligan) and religious faith (James W. Fowler) begin with simple, concrete, and self-serving motives and develop to abstract concepts of transcendent goodness achieved by those who put ego needs aside and work for eternal values, such as human rights, world health, and world peace.

Psychoanalyst Michael Fordham arrived at his theory of personality through years of observing infant behavior. His work illuminates Jung's emphasis on genetic factors and differing archetypal influences on a person from the beginning of life. Far from being formless, passive "blank slates," newborns come into the world with skills for interacting with the environment, according to Fordham. Their interactions are unique and call forth responses from the mothering person which vary from personality to personality. Each infant/mother pair is unique. (Fordham, *Children as Individuals*.)

Psychological research into personality theory has been able to mathematically isolate personality factors which are innate (as opposed to learned), as well as a few universal traits all persons possess to some degree. As Jung intuited, it has been established through research into personality factors that our place on the introversion/extroversion behavioral continuum is one of several factors established before birth, and it is usually stable throughout life.

9

The Opus: Finding the Spirit In Matter

What differentiates Jung's individuation from other programs of self-knowledge? It is the attending to emotionally crippling unconscious complexes. Many programs of self-actualization depend on a conscious decision to improve one's awareness, but without taking unconscious complexes into account, we are never able to be objective in our judgment of the information we receive via the unconscious. Not only conscious reason, but unconscious biases must be considered.

● ● ●

The mystery religions often began with ritual disrobing and divestiture as the beginning of sacrifice. This ritual still exists symbolically today in secular ceremonies—the black robe of graduation, the military uniform and haircut; and in religious ceremonies, the white robe of baptism, the lifted veil of marriage, the priestly collar. On a deeper level this can been seen symbolically as an emptying process, the emptying of the ego and the emptying of the Self into the ego.

Edinger writes:

> ...from the internal standpoint, the image of undressing... refers to the extraction of the soul, to the process of putrefaction. Clothes can signify the body or the particular incarnation out of which an individual is living. Thus if one dreams that clothes are removed and one is naked, it can mean that the naked, essential psyche is being brought into visibility. (Edinger, *The Mysterium Lectures*, p. 68.)

Jung was influenced by the example of the three stages of individuation from the alchemist Gerhard Dorn's *Theatricum Chemicum*. About the first stage Jung wrote:

> This preliminary step, in itself a clear blend of Stoic philosophy and Christian psychology, is indispensable for the

differentiation of consciousness. "The Conjunction," CW
14, par. 672.)

The world as we see it usually is preoccupied with the first stage of
individuation, or as Dorn called it, the first coniunctio. Edinger says
that in the 15th century:

> God fell out of heaven and into the psyche... the collective
> projection of the deity into the realm of religious dogma
> was withdrawn. It was a slow process. What we saw then
> was a collective inflation, a vast increase of ego energy that
> manifested itself everywhere... a great expansion of human
> consciousness on the ego level... paid for by a progressive
> loss of connection to the transpersonal dimension. (Eding-
> er, *Science of the Soul*, p. 11.)

Awareness of the loss of connection to the transpersonal dimension
is not fully conscious in most people, but is felt in a pervasive dissat-
isfaction and striving for something, often something unobtainable.
When attended to, it motivates one to the next stage of individuation.
Jung was moved by the tragedy of loss of connection to the transpersonal that he witnessed in the suffering of so many disillusioned people. As Lionel Corbett writes:

> Jung wanted to make this conscious. He also was able to
> break out of the intellectual straightjacket construed by
> modernity and refute its easy dismissal of the religious as
> sheer superstition. In so doing, he relocated the ground of
> religious experience and spirituality in everyday life. (Cor-
> bett, *Psyche and the Sacred*, p. xi.)

The first stage of individuation leads to consciousness of the loss,
though we may be far from understanding what the loss is about and
being able to fill it.

The second stage is described by Dorn:

> At length the body is compelled to resign itself to, and
> obey, the union of the two that are united (soul and spirit).
> That is the wondrous transformation of the Philosophers,
> of body into spirit and of the latter into body, of which
> there has been left to us by the sages the saying, "Make
> the fixed volatile and the volatile fixed." (Dorn, quoted by
> Jung in "The Conjunction," CW 14, par. 685.)

Edinger explains that wholeness, which is in the first stage a kind of abstract realization, is brought into full-blooded reality in the second stage, so that one lives it out fully in everyday life.

In Jung's *Red Book* we can see the methods of active imagination as Jung used it with himself. Barbara Hannah in her book *Active Imagination* and Robert Johnson in his *Inner Work* have also clearly explained the method.

The third stage is transformative. Like a veil lifted, a rock rent to pour forth new life, a chasm crossed to new vistas, a new consciousness opens into a world of much larger dimensions than was imagined. Jung wrote, "...no one knows how the paradoxical wholeness of man can ever be realized." ("The Conjunction," CW 14, par. 680.)

The paradoxical nature of the Self/Nothingness is characteristic of the religions of Asia and the mystical traditions of Christianity, Judaism, and Islam. The Catholic Church continues to reject its mystics as it has from the time of the Inquisition to the present, as observed in the dismissal of priest Matthew Fox from the Dominican Order.

Professor David Tacey identifies the difference between transcendence as numinous or holy and transcendence at the psychological dimension: To those who believe that transcendence consists of a feeling of inner peace and fullness, as when communing with nature, he says:

> We cannot water down the numinous so that it just means feeling good about the bodily functions; that's what the New Age movement does, i.e., regards a good sunset as a "spiritual experience." The numinous only takes place when we recognize the intrusion of a different order of reality into this one, a thinning of the veil, such that a divine reality is impacting on the human. The sense of feeling good about a sunset... is an entirely human endeavor, on this side of the veil. (Tacey, letter posted on the online discussion forum, The International Association for Jungian Studies, September, 2008, http://www.jungianstudies.org.)

Exploring the numinous leads us beyond psyche and beyond form. David Miller, philosopher and professor of religion, has written on the relationship between Jung's Self and the No-self of Asian philosophy. He notes Jung's acknowledgement that he can find no center in the unconscious and that the ideal center is a "dream of totality," defining the known by the unknown, as alchemy says, *ignotum per ignotius*. (David

Miller, "Nothing Almost Sees Miracles.") Analyst Stan Marlan considers this no-self in the alchemical image of the Black Sun and explores the image in its many permutations in his book. (Marlan, *The Black Sun*.)

While any of us is capable of numinous experiences, in order to grasp the nature of that dimension of psyche, we depend on reports of mystics and contemplatives. John Dourley (in "Jung, Some Mystics, and the Void") describes void states as an identity with divinity, in a nothingness devoid of form and of all urgency to form. In the description of mystics, annihilation of will and intellect is the experience of the return to nothing. These experiences indicate a dimension of psyche that precedes or goes beyond the archetypal. Self-loss in the nothingness is the source of wisdom which can bring universal compassion into human consciousness; no other could be excluded from the totality that is the divine emptiness. (Ashton, "Evocations of Absence.")

> Now this soul has fallen from love into nothingness, and without such nothingness she cannot be the all. (Marguerite Porete, quoted by Dourley, "In the End It All Comes to Nothing," p. 1.)

Analyst and priest Sue Crommelin sees the image of the barren womb in so many Biblical stories of transformative events as a metaphor for the silent place in the soul receptive to the Nothing. The coming of the Christ into the womb of Mary repeats the image of the paradoxical presence/no-presence. Crommelin (from a Christmas sermon) notes that the place of "nothing" in the soul is honored by Thomas Merton in the following excerpt as "le pointe vierge" (the virgin point), which he called the "last, irreducible, secret center of the heart where God alone penetrates":

> There is, at the center of our being, a point of nothingness which is untouched by sin and illusion, a point of pure truth, a point or spark which belongs entirely to God, which is never at our disposal, but from which God disposes of our lives; it is inaccessible in the fantasies of our own mind or the brutalities of our own will. This little point of nothingness and of absolute poverty is the pure glory of God written in us. (Crommelin, *Sermon*.)

Gundry calls this the "still-point." Poet Denise Levertov captures the experience of holiness in the everyday things, calling it "the authentic," "marvelous truth," and "terrible joy" in her poem "Matins."

In the Kabir poem at the end of Chapter 9, I have substituted the word "person" in the last sentence, for "man" in Bly's version.

10

Inner and Outer

Fifty years ago a famous writer, Alan Watts, reported that depth psychology was increasingly out of touch with "the science of human behavior." He felt too much stress had been laid on "the unconscious and its archetypal images." He felt it was being replaced by forms of psychotherapy which were more social and interpersonal. (Watts, *Psychotherapy East and West.*) I disagree with Watts. For one thing, he did not understand Jungian psychotherapy, which unequivocally values the social and interpersonal; second, since he wrote that, advancements in science are now confirming the critical importance of the unconscious, archetypal images, and other findings of depth psychology.

Watts does deserve credit for showing that we Jungians have done a poor job of communicating our philosophies and methods. We talk too much to ourselves and not enough to the public. Some Jungian psychoanalysts (for example, Jean Shinoda Bolen, Harry Wilmer, Clarissa Pinkola Estés, James Hillman, James Hollis, Andrew Samuels, Daryl Sharp, Marion Woodman, and others) have tried to correct that and have contributed much to the public's understanding of Jung through their widely popular books and presentations. Authors Michael Vannoy Adams, David Miller, David Rosen, Susan Rowland, David Tacey, and others try to raise awareness in academia. Still, distortion of and prejudice against Jung's writing abounds. That is my concern.

LAGNIAPPE

II

Two Halves of Life

Besides Jacobi's *The Way of Individuation*, see also David Hart, "The Classical Jungian School." (Young-Eisendrath and Dawson, eds., *The Cambridge Companion to Jung*, pp. 89-100.)

In addition to union of the opposites, Jung stressed developing the "inferior functions." This is based on his typological theory of personality. Assuming we favor one or two functions in our personality (intuition, sensation, thinking, and feeling, as introverts or extroverts), eventually the psyche demands that we become conscious of the others. The acting-out of this principle unconsciously often appears as a "mid-life crisis."

The study of typology is very useful in understanding the individuation process and also in negotiating between couples and organizations. By giving us a handle on different psychological tendencies and approaches to reality, it fosters an approach to otherness that is tolerant and curious, not antagonistic.

Corbett addresses the relationship of personality type to spiritual preferences. (Corbett, *Psyche and the Sacred*.)

12

Sexual Identity

Jung believed that thought, decisions, and active behavior are fundamentally based on images. This is now supported by neuroscience:

> ...not all (organisms) have mental phenomena... Some have both behavior and cognition. Some have intelligent actions but no mind... having a mind means that an organism forms mental representations which can become images, be manipulated in a process called thought, and eventually influence behavior by helping predict the future, plan accordingly and choose the next action...a neural representation, which in turn becomes an image we each experience as belonging to us. (Damasio, *Descartes' Error*, p. 90.)

The recognition of a self (note: small "s") is now thought to be an experience of embodied mental and emotional representations that form a consistent perspective, rooted in a relatively stable biological state of a well-structured organism, and fully interactive with a physical and social environment. In the words of a neuroscientist:

> The truly embodied mind I envision, however, does not relinquish its most refined levels of operation, those constituting its soul and spirit. From my perspective, it is just that soul and spirit, with all their dignity and human scale, are now complex and unique states of an organism. Perhaps the most indispensable thing we can do as human beings, every day of our lives, is remind ourselves and others of our complexity, fragility, finiteness and uniqueness. And this is, of course, the difficult job, is it not: to move the spirit from its nowhere pedestal to a somewhere place, while preserving its dignity and importance; to recognize its humble origin and vulnerability, yet still call upon its guidance. (Damasio, *Descartes' Error*, p. 252.)

An in-depth discussion of the current thinking on the subject of sex, gender, and psychological identity in relation to Analytical Psychology's terms, Anima and Animus, is found in Polly Young-Eisendrath's Chapter 11, "Gender and Contrasexuality" in *The Cambridge Companion to Jung.*

Susan Rowland's work contributes to the current understanding of feminine/masculine principles in contemporary literature and philosophy. (Rowland, *Jung as a Writer.*) For example, see her comparison of Jung and Derrida with regard to creation myths in Casement and Tacey's *The Idea of the Numinous.*

To read more about the attitude toward the feminine in Freud and Jung and about how the Greek god Dionysus figures in progressive psychoanalytic ideas, see James Hillman's *The Myth of Analysis.*

Hillman describes how Anima/Animus constellate each other in familiar examples:

> At the very moment of a new psychological move, we hear animus voices driving us from it by spiritualizing the experience into abstractions, extracting its meaning, carrying it into actions, dogmatizing it into general principles, or using it to prove something. Where anima is vivid, animus enters. Similarly, when at work intellectually, or in spiritual meditation, or where courage is screwed to the sticking place, then anima invades with images and fear, with distractions of attachments and connections, telephoning, natural urges, suicidal despairs, or disturbing with ever deepening questions and puzzling unknowns. Moved by a new idea or spiritual impetus, anima is right there, wanting to make it personal, asking, "How does it relate?" and "What about me?" These torturing incursions of soul into spirit into soul are the syzygy in action. This is the coniunctio...The job is to keep spirit and soul distinct (the spirit's demand) and to keep them attached (the demand of the soul). (Hillman, *Anima: An Anatomy of a Personified Notion*, pp. 182-183.)

Jungian psychoanalyst Jane Wheelwright wrote, "My contention is that the animus and anima are not consistently integrated except in old age. This means the self includes both femaleness and maleness equally. Therefore I perceive androgyny as a self symbol, in the sense that we formerly used the hermaphrodite as a self symbol." (She is referring to the hermaphrodite in Plato and alchemical texts.) (Wheelwright, *For Women Growing Older*, p. 7.)

In *Animus Aeternus*, Chapter 5, "Animus Development," and Chapter 6, "Animus in the Body," relevant issues in women's development are discussed. (McNeely, *Animus Aeternus*, pp. 58-83.)

The research of Paul McLean on the tripartite brain can be found online. Also, it is discussed in *The Biology of Transcendence* by Joseph Chilton Pearce.

Jean Bolen's books, *Goddesses in Every Woman* and *Gods in Every Man*, are lively ways to experience the contrasexual archetypes, Anima and Animus, as they play out in our lives.

13

Relationship to the Collective

Jung believed that by the process of individuation, individuals would make a significant difference in raising the consciousness of the collective many. As citizens of the world, we can follow the example of Andrew Samuels, a Jungian analyst who has spent his life championing human rights and political activism and who continues to inspire us to political and public discourse. The co-founder of "Psychotherapy and Counselors for Social Responsibility," Samuels has authored many books, including *The Plural Psyche*; *The Political Psyche*; and *Politics on the Couch: Citizenship and the Internal Life.*

Others articulating the importance of the political psyche are:

Bernstein, J. *Power and Politics: The Psychology of Soviet-American Partnership*, 1985.

Odajnyk, W. *Jung and Politics: The Political and Social Ideas of C.G. Jung.* New York: New York University Press, 1976.

Alschuler, L. "Jung and Politics" in *The Cambridge Companion to Jung*, Young-Eisendrath and Dawson, eds.

In his article "Jung and Politics," Alschuler shows how the individuation of a person contributes to his or her political development. He concludes that development moves towards an attitude he calls "conscientization," or critical consciousness, and that accomplishment of consciousness contributes to the values of a democracy.

Physicist Smolin wrote on the dangers of "Group-think" to creative scientists. He maintains that true creativity can only be reached in going beyond the need to be a pawn of consensus and in refusing to stay within a rigid circle that the collective has drawn around one. (Smolin, *The Trouble with Physics*.)

Marsha Linehan, a specialist in treatment of Borderline Personality Disorders, suggests that the increase in chaotic families is related to the increase of Borderline Personality Disorder. The borderline personal-ity's emotionality collides with a societal standard of intolerance for strong emotion. Our society rewards differentiation, self-discipline, and independence and separation at the expense of relatedness and emo-tional mirroring. Linehan's cognitive-behavioral treatment requires immersion in a therapeutic environment which removes the patient from overstimulation and rejection. The effects that Linehan ascribes to "individuation" do not refer to Jung's model but have similar concerns about a culture divorced from its instinctual roots. (Linehan, *Cognitive-Behavioral Treatment of Borderline Personality Disorder*.) In such a culture, emotionally sensitive persons have an especially hard time finding their ground of being, while the insensitive more easily assume power.

In discussing kinds of power, Hillman suggests that we revise the idea of growth into a more mature notion of progress. Rather than rewarding power gained by acquisitions, manipulation, and personal dominance, Hillman lists kinds of growth that represent a different psychological attitude towards power: deepening, intensification (for example, in enthusiasm, dedication, and love), shedding, repetition (as in ritual and care), and emptying. (Hillman, *Kinds of Power*, pp. 45-65.)

In an essay, "The Imagination of Air and the Collapse of Alchemy," Hillman proposes that the inventions and discoveries of chemistry and technology since the Enlightenment require us to examine our biases of subjectivity and recognize that the soul is extroverting through the imagination of airy elements (think electronics and cyberspace). (Hill-man, "The Imagination of Air and the Collapse of Alchemy," pp. 273-333.) These happenings in science demand that we adapt a psychic attitude that honors, rather than denies, the transposition of soul from self to public world and materialization as psychological events in the Anima Mundi. This is obvious in the rapid increase in popularity of internet and cell phone communication.

Following that theme in the discussion of the effect of technology on the soul, see Glen Slater's essay, "Cyborgian Drift: Resistance is not Futile," and Wolfgang Giegerich's essay, "The Burial of the Soul in Tech-nological Civilization" both in *Psyche and Nature*, Vol. 1, *Spring Journal* 75, 2006. Slater proposes the useful image of an immune system in dealing with the problems of a bloodless technical society:

> Whether or not we end up as cyborgs will depend on rec-ognizing what drives us forward and finding ways to re-

imagine our relationship to technology as it unfolds. It is vital that we maintain an awareness of undercurrents and archetypal contents that arise in the form of compensating images. Insights derived from the imagination function as antibodies in the collective psyche, preventing certain viruses from completely taking over the system. If there are enough antibodies, enough instinctual, gut-level reactions, if there's a small critical mass of awareness in different disciplines and the culture at large, it may be enough to alter an otherwise blind course. (Slater, "Cyborgian Drift: Resistance is not Futile," p. 191)

Will we continue blindly indulging our addiction to technology in the guise of "progress"? Or will our gut-level aversion to having machines replace intimacy immunize us to the cyborg virus? While we think we are being individualistic in the power we hold with our phones and computers that traverse space, we are in danger of being caught in compelling collective webs of useless information and time-consuming complexes. Their seduction is very subtle.

John Philip Sousa was present at the beginning of recorded music. While the technology helped to popularize his music, he expressed his regret about the invention. He predicted that recorded music would replace the importance of musical expression to the individual person, and the human body would not be called upon to sing and improvise musically.

What young people do not see is how much we now bypass and ignore other parts of the body besides eye, ear, and brain in our entertainment choices, which consume so many hours of living. We do not know what effect this is having on our health and immune systems, but we do know that obesity and chronic diseases, as well as depression, are widespread. Studies show that today's youth are seriously less developed and sensitive to fine sensations in many areas (sounds, colors, word meanings, descriptive vocabulary, and so on) than were previous generations. (Pearce, *The Biology of Transcendence.*)

Does astrology have anything to say about our future as a species? The precession of the equinoxes resulting in the arrival of the two-thousand-year age of Aquarius (beginning around 2000 CE, following the age of Pisces) was predicted by astrologers to bring with it transformative movement in social relations. This suggests that we may be able to use technology to increase human values and soul-making rather than lose our souls in the pursuit of airy, superficial encounters that, having lost touch with the earthy and physical, can only masquerade as intimacy.

The Aquarian movement is expected to raise our consciousness toward greater tolerance and compassion. Richard Tarnas writes about the events of the sixties in view of astrological alignments:

> These reflections are, of course, all anticipated by Jung's understanding of the collective unconscious, but the evidence set forth in this book introduces a certain specificity, and perhaps a more explicit cosmic ground, to the Jungian perspective. (Tarnas, *Cosmos and Psyche*, p. 203.)

Tarnas, respected by many, discredited by some as "pseudo-scientist," writes that Jung's psychology, with its emphasis on the unpredictable, autonomous, and ultimately spiritual nature of the unconscious in its interaction with the conscious ego, was itself part of a cultural awakening reflective of the Uranus-Neptune square of the 1950s. (*Cosmos and Psyche*, p. 403.) One interpretation of individuation is that it liberates us from our horoscope, as the soul determines its fate, transforming the alignment of energy from the astrological influences. But if the age of Aquarius promotes tolerance and compassion, the individuation process should be abetted by the heavenly dynamics, and Pythagoras will smile in his grave.

14

World Cultures

The question of individuation in societies that value non-competitive community is complex. Young-Eisendrath discusses this in terms of disidentifying with the persona. Typically, in large democracies which value diversity, people encounter conflict, which increases neurosis but also motivates self-awareness and individuation. In communities that follow collective traditions, there is less discomfort and more opportunity for orderly development, and, consequently, less incentive toward self-awareness. (Young-Eisendrath and Dawson, eds., *The Cambridge Companion to Jung*.)

What many of the colonizing societies did not recognize was that the definitions of progress and "the good life" as defined by technologically oriented Western countries is not more desirable to the "undeveloped" peoples, at least not until their cultures have been decimated and they require help to survive. The "progressive" usually barges in with little knowledge of history and an inability to see the fine points of the established culture: its traditions, nuances of language, and sensitivity to information that lies outside the intruder's awareness. Most importantly, the intruder is likely to overlook the fact that he navigates from an entirely different set of values about what is important in life. Jung suggested that "primitive people" were superior to their colonizers in areas of consciousness that had been lost to "civilized" societies.

In *The Principle of Individuation*, Stein envisions the individuation of traditions and political forces within nations and cultures. Using the example of North and South America, he illustrates how engaging cultural differences, without being demeaning or showing prejudice, could result in greater wholeness for both groups. (Stein, *The Principle of Individuation*.)

To those critics who see psychoanalysis as a retreat from reality, consider one feature of Jung's thought that is eminently practical in working out one of civilization's greatest current threats—global terrorism and the potential destruction of society through fundamentalism and religio-political world wars. Because Jung's viewpoint encompasses both the secular and the sacred, it is equipped to address and correct the split between secular and sacred which is the heart of the problem of religious fundamentalism, a major threat to world peace. On the issue of religious fundamentalism and the potential within Jung's psychology for mitigating the split between secular and sacred positions, see Roderick Main's "Numinosity and Terror: Jung's psychological revision of Otto as an aid to engaging religious fundamentalism." (Casement and Tacey, *The Idea of the Numinous*.)

An understanding of how the Self is projected in god-images enables those outside a sect to be more respectful and tolerant of extremist attitudes. By this I do not mean being passive or submissive in the face of dangerous hostility, but rather approaching extremism humanely and sanely. Jung shows us how to be sane in the presence of insanity, an approach that he and those of us who have lived and worked in the hidden back wards of hospitals have tried to practice.

15

Individuation: Heroic and Mercurial

Sanford Drob has articulated how Archetypal Psychologies insist on returning to meaning and the soul through the soul's language of dreams, myths, and experiences of chaos and multiplicity. This they have done in spite of the field of psychology's focus on cognition and behavior, models from cybernetics and biology, and the preoccupation with normalcy and unity of the Self that encourages pinning the psyche down to interpretation and operationalism. (Marlan, *Archetypal Psychologies*, pp. 152-168.)

We are only touching on a vast cultural evolution in this sketchy way, to open the door to a library of studies on the subject. To begin with one small area of ethics, see the conversations about Immanuel Kant and Emmanuel Levinas, a teacher of Derrida. (Chalier, *What Ought I To Do?*) Similarities and differences in the way that Kant and Levinas conceive of the basis of morality reflect the shift in cultural attitudes from universal principles (Kant) to particular human relationships (Levinas). Both see the desire to do good as fundamentally present in human nature, but while Kant thinks moral awareness is an innate principle that humans struggle to maintain in the face of natural selfishness, Levinas, a contemporary ethicist, thinks morality is a response to seeing the plight of other distressed humans.

An evolutionary step took place when Carole Gilligan transposed Lawrence Kohlberg's work on the development of moral consciousness. Gilligan noted that Kohlberg's model assumed that an ethical stance could be assumed to be universally correct, when actually it was biased toward a masculine style. She showed that there could be contrasting understandings of right behavior, reflecting differences in priority between feminine and masculine values. (Gilligan, *In a Different Voice*.)

Since the "Decade of the Brain," the 1990s, we now have neurological facts to elucidate much of human activity. Here is Antonio Damasio's exposition of ethical behavior and brain functions:

Both "high-level" and "low-level" brain regions, from the prefrontal cortices to the hypothalamus and brain stem, cooperate in the making of reason...The fact that acting according to an ethical principle requires the participation of simple circuitry in the brain core does not cheapen the ethical principle. The edifice of ethics does not collapse, morality is not threatened, and in a normal individual the will remains the will. What can change is our view of how biology has contributed to the origin of certain ethical principles arising in a social context, when many individuals with a similar biological disposition interact in specific circumstances...neither anguish nor the elation that love or art can bring about are devalued by understanding some of the myriad biological processes that make them what they are. Our sense of wonder should increase before the intricate mechanisms that make such magic possible. Feelings form the base for what humans have described for millennia as the human soul or spirit. (Damasio, *Descartes' Error*, pp. vii-xx.)

Susan Rowland recognizes the problem of "fixing" concepts in time, as opposed to leaving concepts open to be placed in context. She says of Jung's autobiography:

"Memories, Dreams, Reflections" is suspended between the desire to assert "concepts" and the realization that such language is itself a barrier to Jung's understanding of the psyche. (Rowland, *Jung as a Writer*.)

This is clearly the case here, where we are trying to clarify concepts at the risk of concretizing and thereby damaging the experience.

James Hillman initiated Archetypal Psychologies as an approach to Jung's psychology, which emphasized the flexibility of the psyche and the relativity of the ego. Hillman was moved by impatience toward a psychological attitude that asked its followers to be "better" instead of "changing" and "fluid." He noted that analysis often was limited to the head, not the whole person. Some Jungians tended to focus on dreams and fantasies and were not able to look at how the inner life related to the whole personality and lifestyle. What's more, "trying" to relate to a Self could be interpreted as working to please a god or some spiritual judge, just the opposite of the notion of individuation.

Hillman was concerned that, on the other hand, some developmental psychologists were too literal; they tended to ignore innate personality factors that did not depend on personal history for explanation. Although early influences are important, we cannot explain everything about the person we come to be by looking at the way we were raised and treated in childhood. Neither can we limit ourselves with the belief that early experiences *determine*, rather than *influence*, our behavior.

Donald Kalsched's work on early trauma counts developmental influences strongly but also recognizes archetypal influences in recovery from trauma. (Kalsched, *The Inner World of Trauma*.) As a clinician, he sets an example of working at the three dimensions of individuation: the physical, psychological, and transcendent.

Mary Watkins objects to the tendency of developmentalists to treat "imagination" as secondary to reason or as an internalization of external figures. She stresses that "imagination" is an innate psychological function which should be respected and considered on its own terms, not relegated to a subordinate or superordinate position in some hierarchical scheme of psychic faculties. (Watkins, *Invisible Guests*.)

The linear model is only one model of growth. We can approach psychological growth in terms of a circular process of birth-death-rebirth (Murray Stein), the eternal recurrence (Nietzsche and Vico), dialectical assertion-negation-identification (Hegel, Giegerich), or the unpredictable psychic movement that initiates, not from a consistent center, but from any number of archetypal vortices (Hillman, Adams).

Some theorists even question whether ego integrity is a prerequisite to the experience of the Self. Certainly we can experience Self-images and inclinations without ego mediation at any stage of life. The question is whether the effects of Self-awareness can be realized and sustained consciously without a stable ego. Judith Stevens-Long notes that contemporary philosophical, historical, and anthropological perspectives suggest that integrity as an ideal is inconsistent with current research in identity formation. She would argue that psychic movement may originate from any archetype at any level of ego consciousness. Is there more than one developmental path to transcendence? Her conclusion is that the Self is not the synthesizer of experience, but rather the interpreter. "It is too soon to adopt one particular point of view about the nature and direction of optimal development... Profound experiences of disintegration can play an important role in a maturing adult personality." (Young-Eisendrath and Miller, eds., *The Psychology of Mature Spirituality*, p. 166.)

In that same volume, John Beebe contrasts the impossible goal of individuation (a "utopian ideal of personality as a continuous state of consciousness in which no characterologic defenses are evident") with the ideal goal of leaving no part of the Self as split-off and inaccessible to dialogue with the ego. "It is the continuing fate of any human being to experience at least some psychopathology in which split-off complexes set up 'a shadow-government of the ego' or what Jungians often call a state of 'possession by complexes.' What actually individuates is not the total personality, with its inevitable blind spots, but the willingness of the person being analyzed to face them." (Beebe in *The Psychology of Mature Spirituality,* Young-Eisendrath and Miller, eds.)

16

Elitism and Exceptions

"Only those individuals can attain to a higher degree of consciousness who are destined to it and called to it from the beginning, i.e., who have a capacity and an urge for higher differentiation," said Jung. ("On the Psychology of the Unconscious," CW 7, par. 198.)

And then Edinger confuses us with this statement, "We cannot be certain whether we are observing another's individuation, or our own individuation, or perhaps Jung's individuation working through us!" (Edinger, *Science of the Soul*, p. 70.)

Samuels writes that Jung says:

> "before individuation can be taken as a goal, a necessary minimum of 'adaptation' to collective norms must be first attained" (CW 6, para 760). This might mean that individuation is only for those with "strong egos," with good social adaptation and who are functioning genitally. This suggests that individuation is for an elite, and Jung may be able to justify this with his view that nature, after all, is aristocratic (CW 7, paras 198, 236; CW 17, paras 343, 345). Jung refers to people having a "vocation" for individuation. (CW 17, para 300).... "Only the man who can consciously assent to the power of the inner voice becomes a personality." But he goes on to say that the necessary task is to translate the vocation into one's own individual reality (thereby, incidentally, validating the part played by the ego in individuation).
>
> But the use of the word vocation and many other references equating individuation with a religious or spiritual attitude can lead to conceiving individuation as a mystical summons rather than a psychological necessity and process. Individuation does imply an acceptance of what lies beyond the individual, of what is simply unknowable but not unfelt. In that sense individuation is a spiritual calling but, as the realization of the fullness of a personality,

> it is a psychological phenomenon. A search or quest for individuation grips many people and the process itself is sometimes symbolized as the grail rather than the grail as its goal. (Samuels, *Jung and the Post-Jungians*, pp. 110-111.)

Samuels is clarifying that individuation is not necessarily to be regarded in the spiritual dimension; searching the unknowable can be seen as a purely psychological process. Whether one sees it as a spiritual or purely psychological one is a matter of intention and temperament. (For the influence of personality on spirituality, see Corbett, *Psyche and the Sacred*.)

> One danger of an immense involvement with the inner world and its fascination with images is that it may lead to a narcissistic preoccupation. Another danger would be to consider all manifestations, including antisocial activities and even psychotic breakdowns as justifiable results of an individuation process. (Samuels, Shorter, and Plaut, eds., *A Critical Dictionary of Jungian Analysis*, p. 78.)

Inflation occurs when the ego assimilates the Self and does not maintain an identity of humility and questioning. In his autobiography, Jung wrote that in seeking individuation, there is no guarantee that we will not "fall into peril" and choose a deadly road.

Ancients respected the power of the Self as of a god or gods. Moderns do not recognize the power of the Self, but are still subject to it and unwitting victims of it.

As for Joyce and analysis, a wealthy American patroness of the arts, Edith Rockefeller McCormick, became Joyce's benefactor in Zurich. She admired Jung and offered to pay for Joyce to be analyzed by him, but Joyce refused. He wrote disparagingly of psychoanalysis, describing Jung as the Swiss Tweedledum and Freud the Viennese Tweedledee.

17

Beyond the Depressive Position

Now humankind has the power to destroy the world; psychology must articulate to the public whatever it can about constructive intimacy, lest we exterminate our own species and others as well. Jungian psychology proposes finding a standpoint outside of our personal needs, beyond self-serving egoism, in order to know how to achieve constructive intimate relationships. In psychoanalysis we learn to remove the unholy attachments we have to our shadow issues and complexes so as to better understand and relate to ourselves, our families, and our friends and lovers. We learn about unnecessary and necessary suffering and about the contentment in being held by universal, positive forces. Through the consistent presence of the analyst, we reap the rewards of being attended with constancy and compassion. In such a container, as in an alchemical vessel, we transform.

Samuels lists some important issues in which Jung functioned as a precursor to recent developments in post-Freudian psychoanalysis. (Young-Eisendrath and Dawson, eds., *The Cambridge Companion to Jung*, pp. 1-13.) His excellent analysis serves to buttress the reasons why Jung's contributions deserve greater recognition in all schools of psychology and psychiatry today. I will quote two of Samuels's issues:

> While Freud's Oedipal psychology is father-centered and is not relevant to a period earlier than about the age of four, Jung provided a mother-based psychology, in which influence is traced back much earlier, even to pre-natal events. For this reason he may be seen as a precursor of the work of Melanie Klein, of the British School of object-relations theorists such as Fairbairn, Winnicott, Guntrip, and Balin, and, given the theory of archetypes..., of Bowlby's ethologically inspired work on attachment. (Young-Eisendrath and Dawson, eds., *The Cambridge Companion to Jung*, p. 4.)

Later Samuels writes:

> There is a distinction between norms of adaptation, them-
> selves a microcosm of societal values, and an ethic which
> prizes individual variation from the norm as highly as, or
> more highly than, individual adherence to the norm. Al-
> though his cultural values have sometimes been criticized
> as elitist, Jung is the great writer on individuation. Psycho-
> analytic writers (Freudian) on these themes include Winni-
> cott, Milner and Erikson. (Young-Eisendrath and Dawson,
> eds., *The Cambridge Companion to Jung*, p. 6.)

For additional discussions of these issues, see Barbara Stephens ("The Return of the Prodigal: the Emergence of Jungian Themes in Post-Freudian Thought") and Michael Eigen ("The Area of Faith in Winnicott, Lacan, and Bion"). Other post-Freudians include Thomas Ogden and James Grotstein, who have demonstrated new approaches to Freudian theory. Grotstein, representing the current openness of Freudian tradition to the spiritual dimension, writes:

> It is my belief that the "transcendent position" represents
> the achievement of meditative-like grace in which one ex-
> periences solitude with a serenity that transcends conflict.
> One has transcended the ontological skirmishes of the
> paranoid-schizoid position and the lugubrious agonies of
> the depressive position and has achieved the capacity for
> mourning, reparation, empathy, tolerance of ambivalence,
> and true love and caring. One must then continue an on-
> tological pilgrimage to the next state, one of solitude with
> enlightenment and serenity where one is at peace with
> oneself and with the world, both internal and external.
> Whereas, when one was unprepared as an infant to con-
> front the Register of the Real (e.g., chaos, beta elements,
> the things-in-themselves, inherent preconceptions, the
> "shadow side of God," the noumenon), one now as an in-
> dividual who has "learned from experience" is privileged
> to be able to achieve serenity, and to be at peace with the
> entire range of the Register of the Real. In its comprehen-
> sive capacity for "at-one-ness," the transcendent position
> reconciles virtually all the "vertices" or cosmic perspectives
> which inform Bion's higher epistemological endeavors, i.e.,
> the scientific, mathematical, spiritual, mystical, noumenal,
> and aesthetic, to which I now add the transcendent. (Grot-
> stein, "Bion's 'Transformation in O,'" p. 10.)

Freud's attitude toward religion has been examined in terms of personality factors in himself as well as the cultural climate of war between religion and science. (Meissner, *On Putting a Cloud in a Bottle*.) Freud's friend, Oskar Pfister, a Lutheran pastor and psychoanalyst, after reading "The Future of an Illusion," wrote *The Illusion of a Future*. Pfister showed that a properly developed religious attitude promoted truthfulness and psychological freedom, rather than the neurotic wish-fulfillment Freud saw.

Romain Rolland, winner of the Nobel prize for literature in 1916, also Freud's friend, told Freud that what Freud was attacking was not religion but the irreducible spiritual element in the psyche. The question is not whether religion is true or false, but how to make sense of something basic in the human experience. This argument might satisfy the philosopher Ludwig Wittgenstein's thesis that our questions about reality have their answers in the way we live our lives.

Some object-relations theorists saw religion as a particular kind of internal object—not the fantasy figures from childhood, but "internal objects derived from a cultural tradition whose function is to give meaning to a person's experience by placing it in a context that encompasses all existence." (Parsons, *Mankind's Attempt to Understand Itself*, p. 27.)

Parsons reiterates Jung's maxim: Both analyst and patient are changed by the analytic experience.

> That inward openness (of the analyst) is what conveys to the patient, however subtly and silently, that he or she is sharing the struggle to understand and to grow with another human being. Every analytic encounter is, for both parties, a meeting that contains as yet undiscovered knowledge and meaning. (Parsons, *Mankind's Attempt to Understand Itself*, p. 31.)

Analysts may have little insight into mystical absorption and theologians little insight into the unconscious, but W.W. Meissner says that theology and psychoanalysis intersect in the inquiry into mystical life. He discusses critical assessments of mystical experience from various psychoanalytic viewpoints, for example: attempts to repair relationship with mother (Moloney); regression to a symbiotic infantile state (Freud); a narcissistic grandiose union with omnipotent object (Bach); a way of neutralizing aggression (Harticollis). He quotes Heinz Kohut as saying that mystical union may express a "cosmic narcissism which has transcended the bounds of the individual." (Meissner, "On Putting a Cloud in a Bottle," p. 543.)

Although Meissner agrees that mystics show a capacity to reach beyond object-relations and narcissism as Kohut suggests, he argues that the mysticism he presents involves a loving union with God, not with the cosmos.

Meissner contends that the mystic is capable of emptying the ego without detriment to the integrity of his/her volitional core of subjectivity by which he/she is able to love. The continuity of self and identity remains intact. He believes that lower levels of contemplation may depend on sublimation and other repressive mechanisms, but something more is required in infused mystical states.

> Even in the highest state of mystical union, God remains hidden and beyond the reach of human finite capacity to know God as he is. But even so the aspect of love as a capacity of the functioning of human will can reach beyond the limits of human knowledge to be united with God. (Meissner, "On Putting a Cloud in a Bottle," p. 554.)

A psychoanalyst in the Freudian tradition, Bion does not give Jung credit, but his ideas express Jungian ideas in different language. Grotstein explains that Bion's "O" is equivalent to Jung's "Self," the eternal void that undermines deterministic certainty with transcendent doubt. What Jung called the function of transcending "imagination," Bion called "intuition":

> Bion joined the ancient tradition of mystics, such as Meister Eckhart..., Ibn Arabi..., Isaac Luria... and the early Christians and Hebrew mystics, particularly the Gnostics... who had discovered that, through asceticism and self-abnegation, one could look inward and find the immanent and incarnate god. (Grotstein, "Bion's 'Transformation in O,'" pp. 2-4.)

Grotstein says:

> I would emphasize Klein's original concept of infant's need to transcend the depressive position, that is, to free itself not only of persecutory anxieties (paranoid position) but also of depressive anxieties (depressive position), to complete mourning and reach the position of solitude and serenity—without objects to contemplate—the transcendent

position.... Thus, in the transcendent position one experiences the quintessence of subjectivity that transcends (for the moment) object relations. It is the apotheosis of solitude and the attainment of serenity. (Grotstein, "Bion's 'Transformation in O,'" p. 7.)

Grotstein reports an interesting vignette: during the time when Bion was analyzing Samuel Beckett, Bion joined Beckett in attending a lecture by Jung at the Tavistock Clinic. "Jung happened to have alluded to a patient whose resistance was due to his refusal to be born. That very interpretation seemed also to apply to Beckett, who thereby overcame his writer's block and thereupon went on to become 'Samuel Beckett' the Nobelist playwright. It remains a mystery why Bion, who obviously appreciated Jung's thinking, never really acknowledged Jung." (Casement and Tacey, *The Idea of the Numinous*, p. xiii.)

In agreement with Jung's theory, Grotstein thought of the unconscious as populated by a numinous subject, the "dreamer who dreams the dream." (Grotstein, *Who is the Dreamer Who Dreams the Dream?*)

Ira Progoff states that, around the time of Otto Rank's death, Rank was writing in *Beyond Psychology* about a new kind of psychology that would turn its attention to "those psychological capacities in the human being by means of which new experiences of the meaning of man's existence can be encountered... The new style of psychology must be one that gives modern man access to resources that are adequate for a spiritual leap going beyond psychology." (Progoff, *Depth Psychology and Modern Man*, pp. 62-63.)

The attitude that we are presenting here is one of openness and accessibility to a more flexible psychology which encourages questions more than answers.

18

Transcendent Traditions: A New Myth

> The religious cultist wants to become unconsciously absorbed in the mysteries, whereas Jung interprets visionary data without falling into either obscurantism or over-confident rationalism. (Gundry, *Beyond Psyche*.)

When we consider the unus mundus, the fact that Jung explored synchronicity always comes up. The "acausal principle," as Jung called synchronicity, fascinates many and is scoffed at by many. I have deliberately omitted a discussion of synchronicity in Part I, as I feel it would take us into philosophical depths that are beyond our scope here. However, I include here a few references for those who want to explore the subject:

> CW 8. "Synchronicity: An Acausal Connecting Principle" and "On Synchronicity."

> Donati, Marialuisa. "Beyond synchronicity: the worldview of Carl Gustav Jung and Wolfgang Pauli." *The Journal of Analytical Psychology*, 2004, 49, 707-728.

> Heisig, James. *Imago Dei: A Study of C.G. Jung's Psychology of Religion*. Lewisburg: Bucknell University Press, 1979.

> Mansfield, Victor. *Synchronicity, Science, and Soul Making*. Chicago: Open Court, 1995.

> Cambray, Joseph. "Synchronicity and emergence," *American Imago*, 2002, 59, 4, pp. 409-14.

Dourley describes Jung's mature position on the relationship to the divine as "the experience of the divine as a deepest dimension of humanity's experience of itself and of nature." Dourley states further, "God approaches humanity entirely from within...those who remain unaware of the fact are ignorant of the dynamics of religious experience." ("Response to Barbara Stephens's 'The Martin Buber–Carl Jung disputations,'" p. 482.) This position is a development beyond the experience of the divine as an alien other. It is reflected in Meister Eckhart's prayer to have his relationship with God (as creator to creature) dissolved through a moment of identity with the Godhead.

About the transformation of God, Stein writes:

> As the ego engages archetypal figures of the unconscious, it induces change and transformation in them. This brings consciousness not only to the individual human so engaged, but also to the archetypal powers that have been called into play. Indeed, "die Göttlichkeit" itself is moved toward greater consciousness. The self and its transcendent ground are therefore evolving, emerging structures in process, not something given, foreordained unmoving and unmovable that might show itself occasionally like a mountain when the fog and mist clear away. (Stein, *Divinity expresses the Self.*)

On the subject of responsibility for finding the divine within, it can be said that Christianity may have encouraged that as well, but the message is ambiguous. Many times Christ taught that the way was hard, that we must knock and the door will be opened, and that the lowly and suffering have the advantage in coming into the kingdom, because they were more realistic and humble in understanding their personal relations with God. Jesus is a Self-figure for many, and gospel music attributes Self-symbols to Jesus, such as "my rock," "my anchor," and "my way." Early Gnostic sects of Christianity were very much religions of personal responsibility and inward searching. When Jesus said we must become as little children, did he mean that we must humbly reflect on our innocence, or that we must blindly accept the teaching of authorities? Since he spoke at a time when there was no organized church, we assume the former. But in Christianity as it is practiced generally today, little effort is placed on knowing oneself, and this is a significant difference from Analytical Psychology and the Mystery Schools. The result is that Christians tend to follow a prescribed way without connecting to the deeper roots of the spirit; looking into our own motives is not encouraged, and the whole area of evil, inside and outside oneself, is not to be explored. (See Scholem, *Alchemy and Kabbalah*, and Bloom, "Is God an Accident?")

19

Transcendent Traditions: Jung and Buddhism

Barry Magid, a psychoanalyst and Zen teacher, believes that the present generation has witnessed Buddhism's finally becoming established in the West. He notes that Buddhism and psychoanalysis can be practiced together, and each can enrich the perspective of the other. Magid describes the difference between psychoanalysis and psychotherapy in that psychoanalysis is not a goal-oriented technique, and therefore, is more like Zen practice. He writes:

> Despite an increasing trend toward the medicalization of all forms of psychotherapy, driven in large part by the cost containment requirements of the managed care and insurance industries, psychoanalysis by its very nature refuses to be time-limited, Symptom-focused, or outcome-oriented. At a time when psychiatry is increasingly being taken over by neurology and psychopharmacology, psychoanalysis continues to define itself in terms of such nonqualifiables as self-esteem, personal meaning, and identity. Its ancestor is not just Hippocrates, who first established the standards for the medical profession, but more importantly Socrates, who led his interlocutors into an open-ended exploration of the nature of the good life. (Magid, *Ending the Pursuit of Happiness*, p. 145.)

Other books on this subject are Magid's *Ordinary Mind: Exploring the Common Ground of Zen and Psychoanalysis* and Jeremy Safran's *Psychoanalysis and Buddhism: An Unfolding Dialogue.*

20

Other Transcendent Traditions

In his study of New Age spiritual traditions, Don Williams cites these resources:

> Eric Caplan, *Mind Games: American Culture and the Birth of Psychotherapy*. Berkeley: U of Cal Press, 98;

> Eli Zaretsky, *Secrets of the Soul: A Social and Cultural History of Psychoanalysis*. New York: Vantage Books, 2004.

Alchemy preoccupied much of Jung's later life. Marie-Louise von Franz, Erich Neumann, and Gershom Scholem were among many who accompanied Jung into the territory of alchemy. More recently, Stanton Marlan, Sanford Drob, Joseph Henderson, Gus Cwik, and Joseph Cambray are among those who have published on the relationship of alchemy to Analytical Psychology.

On the subject of correspondences between Jungian psychoanalysis, alchemy, Kabbalah, and Tarot symbolism, see Irene Gad's *Tarot and Individuation*.

Jung was very much influenced by Jewish mysticism. The Kabbalah, along with pagan and Christian sources, was a prominent influence on alchemy. Also, Jung used "Adam Kadmon" as a Kabbalistic symbol of primordial man to illustrate the process of individuation and transformation through psychoanalysis. (Drob, "Jung's Kabbalistic Visions.")

Other traditions of soul searching, such as that of Mystery Schools, are typically founded on ancient Hebrew philosophical ideas, especially the Kabbalah, and they recognize the importance of the journey-by-intention toward spiritual development. Like individuation and Buddhism, the responsibility for awareness is up to the effort of the student. Most of what has been sifted down to us about Kabbalah comes through the sixteenth century rabbi, Isaac Luria. In experiencing the Lurianic Tree of Life, the student contacts the underlying unity of the whole world of cosmic polarities inwardly, in their positive and negative expressions, as well as the source of all creation which is perfect stillness, the Ein-Sof. The Sephiroth, ten divine traits or archetypes, represent all things in constant flux, changing, breaking apart, and being restored for the purpose of establishing divine unity. Students are given rituals and exercises to elicit the energies of the Sephiroth and the various paths to them that lie on the Tree of Life.

The early Mystery Schools were ambiguous in the sense that some stressed extroverted magical work, while others stressed introverted mystical experience. Jungians appreciate the reflection on archetypal images which the Mystery Schools teach. These images are bound to touch deeply into psyche and open us to more. Attempting an awareness and balance of positive and negative forces is also valued by Jungians. The difference between the Mystery School studies and Jung's individuation is that the Mystery School images which are worked with are established by tradition and presented as a program, not allowed to come spontaneously to awareness. Also, the psychological dimension is not systematically analyzed, as in individuation.

Jungian psychoanalyst Marvin Spiegelman described the period in his professional development when he concentrated on integrating psychoanalysis and body therapy. He worked with Francis Israel Regardie, who combined Wilhelm Reich's technique with methods from his experience as teacher in the mystery school, the Order of the Golden Dawn. With the guidance of Regardie, Spiegelman explored Buddhist meditation, guided imagery, and daily practices of the Kabbalistic meditative method of the Kabbalah's Middle Pillar while continuing the Jungian method of active imagination:

> Unlike what I was led to believe about such combining of practices in my earlier education on the spiritual path of individuation, I did not find these diverse ways of approaching the psyche to cause undue disharmony or damage.... I believe that the active relationship with the psyche, with such methods as active imagination, are of central importance for those who would like to prove empirically for themselves, just what it was that Jung discovered. (Spiegelman, *The Unhealed Healer*, pp. 204-205.)

Like Jung's map of the soul, Kabbalists picture four worlds or dimensions which follow into being after the stillness of Ein-Sof: the first world of the creative urge (God's image of the purpose of the being or thing); the second world of energy patterns (differentiation of the way the being or thing is to be created); the third world of perfect image of the being or thing in our reality; and the fourth world, the physical being or thing as it is actualized. The parallel in the Jungian schema would be the first world, the creative urge; second world, archetypal pattern; third world, universal or collective expression of the image of the archetype; fourth world, particular expression of the image. Kabbalists of some schools follow the soul into the afterlife, as in Tibetan Buddhism, and describe the tasks of passing through the worlds in preparation for reincarnation. Jung gave no images of the afterlife, feeling it was beyond anything he could observe in human behavior and therefore out of his purview. However, in his last years of life, his dreams suggested the continuation of life beyond death.

Like Mystery School methods, many other spiritual programs, such as the Spiritual Exercises of Ignatius Loyola, assign prescribed imagery. Ignatius's images center on the life of Christ. Without the spontaneity of psychic dialogue, it is quite possible that the student does not approach her/his own psychological issues, such as repressed contents, particularly the unpleasant and shameful ones (the shadow). Spiritual transformation is the goal, though the complexes expressed in the physical body and in interpersonal relationships are not necessarily engaged.

Rudolf Steiner's Anthroposophy involved dialogue with the unconscious which resembled Jung's approach. The difference in that case was that Jung understood the contact to be with split-off contents of the psyche which should be subject to evaluation and ego-dialogue, but Steiner took the contacts at face value as spiritual entities and revelations. Steiner recognized two dimensions of the depth of being, the physical and the etheric, or spiritual. "The etheric body of a man is feminine and the etheric body of a woman is masculine... Through man's physical body he stands within the forces of the earth; through his etheric body with the forces of the extra-terrestrial cosmos." (Steiner, *The Course of My Life*, p. 349.)

The assumption of a separate dimension in outer reality is a leap Jung would not take; it is the belief in the objective nature of the beings contacted as "others" (rather than psychic contents) which separates most spiritualists from the Jungian process. This is difficult to distinguish as Jung also refers to the reality of the psyche, and to the contents of the psyche as autonomous. For Jung the ego standpoint is always engaged with the larger psyche as part of a whole. In Jung's estimation, the spiritual beings and contacts or split-off complexes are representative images by means of which the ego contacts the ultimately unfathomable Self. Through coming to know these sub-personalities, the ego glimpses the presence of the One and recognizes its (ego's) partiality. The sub-personalities are not themselves the One. Had the angel Gabriel come to Jung's wife, she may have had a very special son, but he would not have started a religion.

The spiritualism movements suffered from inattention to the psychological dimension; consequently some of its leaders failed to confront the unconscious shadow and became psychotic. As we have seen, touching the Self as we do in transcendent traditions can invite inflation with the energy of the Self. Spiritual leaders are especially vulnerable to being inflated and taken over by power complexes. Psychotherapists are subject to the same problems, which is why they spend so much time and energy in analysis, learning to recognize their unconscious shadow issues. Unanalyzed power complexes ruin many spiritual traditions as factions grow up around certain leaders and split the groups.

In illustrating symbols of transformation, Jung drew upon Islamic mysticism, beginning with "The Cave" Sura of the Koran, which is taken up with the rebirth mystery. Jung relates the symbolism in the Koran to similar symbols in the Mithraic, alchemical, Christian, and Navajo traditions. In Islam, Khidr is born in a cave, is dismembered like the Egyptian god, Osiris, and is a symbol of the Self of higher wisdom which transcends human reason, comparable to Purusha and Atman of Hindu mythology. Jung tells the story of Moses and Khidr and shows that the intuition of immortality is a universal experience of transformation through connection with the unconscious, which is beyond time and space. "The feeling of immortality, it seems to me, has its origin in a peculiar feeling of extension in space and time, and I am inclined to regard the deification rites in the mysteries as a projection of these same psychic phenomena." ("The Psychology of the Child Archetype," CW 9i, par. 249.) Jung notes that the story reflects the passion in the Islamic religion. That passion is what appeared to him to be missing in many twentieth-century churchgoers and what deprived them of contact with the Self.

Murray Stein imagines Christianity as a patient needing healing to mend old splits and prepare for a new phase of development: The message to Christianity would be:

> Open yourself to the unconscious. Honor the dream. Allow the unconscious to smash the cathedral and to show you a larger image of God, because your God is too small and too confined in the boxes of dogma and habit. Recognize that your tribalism is based on wish and projection and is very distorted, having very little or nothing to do with reality. Allow yourself to consider all the other paths to God as equally valid and legitimate, and possibly equally tribal and limited, but do not abandon your own history, and do not think the other traditions can bail you out if you will just learn some new ideas from them. Instead concentrate yourself on your own symbols and your own history, and let your unconscious respond trusting that the God who revealed himself in the beginning will respond with symbols of transformation and renewal. But you must be prepared to take responsibility for these new revelations, to test them by your very best means of interpretation and discernment, not according to what you have already known, but according to what you know you need and have not found. And be ready to be surprised. Above all, be prepared to let God be whole. This is a great risk, but your life depends on it. (Stein, *The Principle of Individuation*, p. 185.)

Classical readings related to this chapter include Rudolf Otto's *The Idea of the Holy*, Richard Wilhelm's *The Secret of the Golden Flower*, and Mircea Eliade's *Shamanism*. Interesting insights into Jung's views on religion can be found by reading his autobiography and "Seven Sermons to the Dead" (appendix to *Memories, Dreams, Reflections*), his *Red Book*, his published letters, and in his collected works, particularly *Answer to Job*.

Jung's map of the psyche found its borders at the archetypal dimension. Jung acknowledged deeper layers, but they cannot be described except as the pleroma in "Seven Sermons to the Dead" or the "central fire." Some people experience a dimension of being that seems to be deeper than the archetypal energies with their opposing images and compensatory movement. This deeper level comprehends the stillness of being before the creative energy begins to move toward actualization. Nothing is articulated. So, perhaps, it goes farther than Jung could go in describing the Self; yet the way of awakening to the psyche and living in the knowledge of the relativity of the ego is very compatible between Analytical Psychology and such intimations of absence, as in mysticism and Buddhism. Still, Jung contended that we could never completely escape the ego during this lifetime; we do continue to care for ourselves as integrated physical bodies, as I believe most mystics would agree.

> For we are in the deepest sense the victims and the instruments of cosmogonic "love." I put the words in quotation marks to indicate that I do not use it in its connotations of desiring, preferring, favoring, wishing, and similar feelings, but as something superior to the individual, a unified and undivided whole. Being a part, man cannot grasp the whole. He is at its mercy. He may assent to it or rebel against it; but he is always caught up by it and enclosed within it. He is dependent on it and is sustained by it. Love is his light and his darkness, whose end he cannot see. "Love ceases not"—whether he speaks with the "tongues of angels" or with scientific exactitude traces the life of the cell down to its uttermost source. Man can try to name love, showering upon it all the names at his command, and still he will involve himself in endless self-deceptions. If he possesses a grain of wisdom he will lay down his arms and name the unknown by the more unknown, ignotum per ignotius—that is, by the name of God. That is a confession of his subjection, his imperfection, and his dependence; but at the same time a testimony to his freedom to choose between truth and error. (Jung, *Memories, Dreams, Reflections,* p. 354.)

21

A Question of Endpoints

Here are some descriptions of outcomes of the individuation process articulated by Jung and a few of his followers:

> **Individuation** means becoming an "individual"... our innermost last and incomparable uniqueness... he does not become selfish... but is merely fulfilling the peculiarity of his nature... a living cooperation of all factors... ("The Relations Between the Ego and the Unconscious," CW 7, par. 266-228.)

> **The individuated ego** "senses itself as the object of an unknown and supraordinate subject... the idea of a self is itself a transcendental postulate which, though justifiable psychologically, does not allow of scientific proof." ("The Relations Between the Ego and the Unconscious," CW 7, par. 405.)

> **Individuation** involves making conscious and peeling away from one's personal sense of self a great deal of unconscious material—all the introjections and identifications, the unconscious identity with objects and people, which have accumulated over a lifetime. This is an ongoing aspect of individuation that is never final, never complete. (Stein, *Journal of Jungian Theory and Practice*, p. 5.)

> **Individuation** can be pictured as a labyrinthine spiral with the Self at the center. (Whitmont, *The Symbolic Quest*, 1978.)

> ...for Nietzsche and Jung, **the goal or height of human health and potential** is the realization of the whole self, which they refer to as the "Ubermensch" and "Self" respectively. This achievement is marked by creativity, which is achieved by the cultivation and balance of all antithetical psychological impulses—both rational and irrational—within the personality, and it is in this sense that I shall re-

fer to the whole self as a union of opposites... (Huskinson, *The Self as Violent Other*, p. 3.)

...we feel summoned by something beyond ourselves to become all of ourselves...the task of **individuation** makes us appreciate the world around us with renewed interest and gratitude. For we see that we are continually offered objects with which to find and release our own particular personality... we see the process going on in others too, and we gain a whole new sense of community, kinship, etc. (Ann Ulanov in *The Cambridge Companion to Jung*, pp. 304-5.)

Experientially, one comes to witness and accept a range of subjective states without blame and with a certain playfulness or lightness of being. The usual outcome of this (*individuation*) process is greater courage, insight, empathy and creativity—means for uniting the opposites, as Jung would say. (Polly Young-Eisendrath in *The Cambridge Companion to Jung*, p. 237.)

... *the therapeutic goal of the coniunctio* would now be experienced as a weakening of consciousness, in the former sense of that notion, rather than an increase of consciousness through "integrating" the anima... A therapy that would move toward this coniunctio would be obliged to stay always within the mess of ambivalence, the comings and goings of the libido, letting interior movement replace clarity, interior closeness replace objectivity, the child of psychic spontaneity replace literal right action...Conscious once meant in English, "knowing together." As we cannot go it alone, we cannot know it alone.... Another is implied, not only because the soul cannot exist without its "other" side, but also because consciousness itself has an erotic, Dionysian component that points to participation. (Hillman, *The Myth of Analysis*, p. 296.)

Speaking of a good ego-self connection:

...an ego that feels itself organically linked to the totality of its nature, often expressed in a feeling of spontaneous self-confidence... a sense that despite the shadow side and whatever weakness there may be, one is essentially and ultimately sound, solid and of worth. If we add the religious dimension of the self as proposed by Jung, we might see self-confidence as also consisting in the conviction that one is in "God's care"...the ego has access to spontaneity and instinct, the experience of inner vitality. (Jacoby, *Individuation and Narcissism*, p. 72.)

Jacoby focuses on traits of empathy, creativity, humor, and wisdom (including acknowledging finiteness) as effects of **individuation**. Empathy is basic to the ability to maintain relationships; it involves projection, introspection, and the ability to better differentiate our own projections from the perceived complex processes of the other. Creativity is a mark of being in touch with the inner sources of liveliness and spontaneity.

Jacoby explains that **completion**—and not perfection—includes accepting our embarrassment, awkwardness, stupidity. It requires a certain degree of self-esteem to accept these sides in one's personality with tolerant humor without feeling devalued as a whole person. Wisdom is the capacity to intellectually and emotionally accept the imperfection inherent in human nature.

Continuing descriptions of end-points:

> **Completion** is not closure... completion is the drive to go on including the other, as failure, darkness, the not known. Since the unconscious is inappropriate territory, completion is a drive, not a fixed state. (Rowland, *Jung as a Writer*, pp. 44-46.)

> ...**individuation** is a potential conversion of apocalypse into deliverance, and vice-versa. (Rowland, *Jung as a Writer*, pp. 44-46.)

> the **individuated person** lives in the world of active imagination; that the ego does not identify with the outer world, nor the inner world, but with the imaginative world— which includes both of the others... it would see underneath the apparent solidity of ordinary reality to the meaning hidden there. It would behold the spiritual powers at play in ordinary life, and it would possess the freedom that perceiving symbolically bestows. (von Franz, in Raff, *Jung and the Alchemical Imagination*, p. 62.)

> Jung offered a spiritual model for the modern world... The main element of this model is the generation of the manifest self... the profound implications of transforming a self are often overlooked, for it is not simply a question

of being more whole, or even more unique. Manifesting a self implies the most intense inner transformation imaginable—the transformation of one's inner nature into that of a divinity. This does not suggest that human nature be left behind, but that it finds its true depths in union with the divine... the divine nature of the human being, hidden beneath the chaotic waters of the unconscious in the latent self, as awakened and pushed toward its own manifestation through the efforts of the ego... Only a thorough study of Jung's writings indicate how deeply he felt this transformation and how he envisioned it. He perceived in the movement toward **individuation** a progressive union of human and divine. (Raff, *Jung and the Alchemical Imagination*, pp. 104-105.)

It is my belief that the "transcendent position" represents the achievement of meditative-like grace in which one experiences solitude with a serenity that transcends conflict. (Grotstein, *Who is the Dreamer Who Dreams the Dream?*, p. 10.)

Individuation can be called by two words:

Open. Gratitude.

BIBLIOGRAPHY

Adams, John. "Sonic Youth," *The New Yorker*, August 25, 2008, 32.

Als, Hilton. "Intruder in the Wings," *The New Yorker*, May 26, 2008.

Alschuler, Lawrence. "Jung and Politics." Lecture given at The International Association for Jungian Studies / International Association for Analytical Psychology conference, Zurich, Switzerland, July, 2008.

Ashton, Paul, ed. *Evocations of Absence: Multidisciplinary Perspectives on Void States*. New Orleans: Spring Journal, Inc., 2007.

Auden, W. H. *Collected Poems*. Edited by Edward Mendelson. New York: Modern Library, 2007.

Austin, James H. *Zen and the Brain*. Boston: MIT Press, 1999.

Bartusiak, Marcia. *Einstein´s Unfinished Symphony*. Washington, D. C.: Joseph Henry Press, 2000.

Bernstein, Jerome. *Power and Politics: The Psychology of Soviet-American Partnership*. Boston: Shambhala Publications, 1989.

_____. *Living in the Borderland: The Evolution of Consciousness and the Challenge of Healing Trauma*. New York: Taylor and Francis Publishers, 2005.

Bloom, Harold. *Jesus and Yahweh: The Names Divine*. New York: Riverhead Books, 2005.

Bloom, Paul. "Is God an Accident?" *The Atlantic Online*. December, 2005, http://www.theatlantic.com/doc/200512/god-accident. Also available in print form.

Bly, Robert. *The Kabir Book*. Boston: Beacon Press, 1971.

Brooke, Roger. "The Fall and Rise of Expertise," *Bulletin of American Academy of Clinical Psychology*, Fall 05/Winter 06, 10, 1, 8-10.

Brooke, Roger. "*Ubuntu* and the Individuation Process: Toward a Multicultural Analytical Psychology," *Psychological Perspectives*, 51:36-63, 2008, 49-50.

Burleson, Blake W., and John Beebe. *Pathways to Integrity: Ethics and Psychological Types*. Gainesville, Florida: Center for Application of Psychological Types, 2001.

Casement, Ann, and David Tacey. *The Idea of the Numinous*. New York: Routledge, 2006.

Chalier, Catherine. *What Ought I To Do? Morality in Kant and Levinas*. Translated by Jane Marie Todd. Ithaca, New York: Cornell University Press, 2002.

Corbett, Lionel. *The Religious Function of the Self.* London: Routledge, 1996.

———. *Psyche and the Sacred: Spirituality Beyond Religion.* New Orleans: Spring Journal Books, 2007.

Crommelin, Sue. Sermon, December 25, 2008.

Dallett, Janet. *When the Spirits Come Back.* Toronto: Inner City Books, 1988.

———. *Saturday's Child: Encounters with the Dark Gods.* Toronto: Inner City Books, 1991.

Damasio, Antonio. *Descartes' Error.* London: Penguin Books Ltd., 1994.

Diamond, Jared. *Collapse: How Societies Choose to Fail or Succeed.* New York: Viking Press, 2005.

Donati, Marialuisa. "Beyond Synchronicity: the Worldview of Carl Gustav Jung and Wolfgang Pauli." *The Journal of Analytical Psychology,* 2004, 49, 707-728.

Douglas, Claire. "The Historical Context of Analytical Psychology." In *The Cambridge Companion to Jung,* edited by Polly Young-Eisendrath and Terence Dawson. Cambridge: Cambridge University Press, 1997, 17-34.

Dourley, John. *A Strategy for a Loss of Faith: Jung's Proposal.* Toronto: Inner City Books, 1992.

———. "Response to Barbara Stephens's 'The Martin Buber–Carl Jung disputations: protecting the sacred in the battle for the boundaries of analytical psychology.'" *The Journal of Analytical Psychology,* 2001, 46, 3, 455-91.

———. "In the End It All Comes to Nothing: The Basis of Identity in Non-Identity." Lecture given at The International Association for Jungian Studies / International Association for Analytical Psychology conference, Zurich, Switzerland, July, 2008.

Dossey, Larry. *Space, Time and Medicine.* Boulder, Colorado: Shambhala Publications, 1982.

Drob, Sanford. "James Hillman on Language: Escape from the Linguistic Prison." In *Archetypal Psychologies: Reflections in Honor of James Hillman,* edited by Stanton Marlan. New Orleans: Spring Journal Books, 2008.

———. "Jung's Kabbalistic Visions." In *Journal of Jungian Theory and Practice* 7, no. 1, http://www.junginstitute.org/pdf_files/JungV7N1p33-54.pdf.

———. "Towards a Kabbalistic Psychology: C.G. Jung and the Jewish Foundations of Alchemy." In *Journal of Jungian Theory and Practice* 5, no. 2, 2003, http://www.junginstitute.org/pdf_files/JungV5N2p77-100.pdf.

_____. "The Mystical Symbol: Some Comments on Ankori, Giegerich, Scholem, and Jung." In *Journal of Jungian Theory and Practice* 7, no. 1, 2005, http://www.junginstitute.org/pdf_files/JungV7N1p25-30. pdf.

Edelman, Gerald and Giulio Tononi. *A Universe of Consciousness: How Matter Becomes Imagination*. New York: Basic Books, 2000.

Eckhart, Meister. *Meister Eckhart: A Modern Translation*. Translated by Raymond Bernard Blakney. New York: Harper and Row, 1941.

Edinger, Edward. *The Creation of Consciousness*. Toronto: Inner City Books, 1984.

_____. *The Mysterium Lectures*. Toronto: Inner City Books, 1995.

_____. *Science of the Soul*. Toronto: Inner City Books, 2002.

Eigen, Michael. "The Area of Faith in Winnicott, Lacan and Bion." In *Relational Psychoanalysis: The Emergence of a Tradition*, edited by Stephen Mitchell and Lewis Aron. Hillsdale, New Jersey: The Analytic Press, 1999.

Ellenberger, Henri. *The Discovery of the Unconscious*. New York: Basic Books, 1970.

Epstein, Mark. *Thoughts Without a Thinker*. New York: Basic Books, 1995.

Feynman, Richard. *The Pleasure of Finding Things Out*. New York: Basic Books, 2005.

Floyd, Keith. "Of Time and the Mind." *Fields Within Fields Within Fields*, 10, Winter, 1973-74.

Fordham, Michael. *Children as Individuals*. London: Hodder and Stoughton, 1969.

Gad, Irene. *Tarot and Individuation*. York Beach, Maine: Nicholas-Hayes, Inc., 1994.

Giegerich, Wolfgang. "The Burial of the Soul in Technological Civilization," Psyche and Nature 1, *Spring Journal* 75, 2006.

Gilligan, Carol. *In a Different Voice*. Boston: Harvard University Press, 1993.

Glass, Richard. "Psychodynamic Psychotherapy and Research Evidence: Bambi Survives Godzilla?" *Journal of the American Medical Association*, October 1, 2008, 300, 1587-1589.

Grinnell, Robert. *Alchemy in a Modern Woman*. Dallas, TX: Spring Publications, 1973.

Grotstein, James S. *Who is the Dreamer Who Dreams the Dream? A Study of Psychic Presences*. Hillsdale, New Jersey: Analytic Press, 2000.

_____. "Bion's 'Transformation in O' and the Concept of the Transcendent Position," 1997, http://www.sicap.it/~merciai/bion/papers/grots. htm.

_____. Foreword to *The Idea of the Numinous*. Edited by Ann Casement and David Tacey. London: Routledge, 2006, xi-xv.

Gundry, Mark. *Beyond Psyche: Symbol and Transcendence in C.G. Jung*. New York: Peter Lang Publishing, 2006.

Hadamard, Jacques. *The Mathematician's Mind*. Princeton, New Jersey: Princeton University Press, 1973.

Hannah, Barbara. *Encounters With the Soul: Active Imagination As Developed by C.G. Jung*. Santa Monica: Sigo Press, 1981.

Hart, David. "The Classical Jungian School." In *The Cambridge Companion to Jung*, edited by Polly Young-Eisendrath and Terence Dawson. Cambridge: Cambridge University Press, 1997, 89-100.

Hawking, Stephen. "Life in the Universe." January, 2009. http://hawking.org.uk.

Hazen, Robert and Trefil, James. *The Physical Sciences*. New York: John Wiley and Sons, 1996.

Hegarty, Antony. *For Today I Am A Boy*. Secretly Canadian. Antony and the Johnsons. Compact disc, 2005.

Henderson, Joseph and Sherwood, Dyane. *Transformation of the Psyche*. New York: Brunner-Routledge, 2003.

Heisig, James. *Imago Dei: A Study of C.G. Jung's Philosophy of Religion*. Lewisburg: Bucknell University Press, 1979.

Hill, Bernice. *Money and the Spiritual Warrior*. Boulder, Colorado: Five Centuries Foundation, 2004.

Hillman, James. *Revisioning Psychology*. New York: Harper and Row, 1976.

_____. "Imagination of Air and the Collapse of Alchemy," *Eranos* 50, 1981, 273-333.

_____. *Anima: An Anatomy of a Personified Notion*. Dallas, TX: Spring, 1985.

_____. "Peaks and Vales: The Soul-Spirit Distinction as Basis for the Differences between Psychotherapy and Spiritual Discipline." *Puer Papers*. Irving, Texas: Spring, 1987.

_____. *The Myth of Analysis*. Evanston, IL: Northwestern University Press, 1992.

_____. *Kinds of Power*. New York: Bantam Doubleday Dell, 1995.

Hoeller, Stephan A. *The Gnostic Jung and the Seven Sermons to the Dead*. Wheaton, Illinois: Theosophical Publishing House, 1982.

Hofstadter, Douglas R. *Gödel, Escher, Bach: An Eternal Golden Braid*. New York: Vintage Books, 1980.

_____. *I Am a Strange Loop.* New York: Basic Books, 2007.

Horgan, John. "Why Freud Isn't Dead," *Scientific American*, Dec., 1996, 106-111.

Huskinson, Lucy. "The Self as Violent Other," *The Journal of Analytical Psychology* 47, no. 3, 2002, 437-458.

_____. *Nietzsche and Jung.* New York: Brunner-Routledge, 2004.

_____,ed. *Dreaming the Myth Onwards.* London: Routledge, 2008.

Jacobi, Jolande. *The Way of Individuation.* New York: Harcourt, Brace, and World, 1967.

Jacoby, Mario. *Individuation and Narcissism.* New York: Routledge, 1990.

James, William. *Varieties of Religious Experience.* New York: Fine Creative Media, 2004.

Jarrett, James. "Schopenhauer and Jung." *Spring Journal.* Dallas: Spring Publications, 1981, 193.

Johnson, Robert. *Inner Work.* New York: Harper and Row, 1986.

Jung, Carl Gustav. *The Collected Works* (Bollingen Series XX). 20 vols. Trans. R.F.C. Hull. Ed. H. Read, M. Fordham, G. Adler, Wm. McGuire. Princeton: Princeton University Press, 1953-1979.

_____. *Memories, Dreams, Reflections.* Ed. Aniela Jaffé. New York: Vintage Books Edition, 1989.

_____, Sonu Shamdasani, Mark Kyburz, and John Peck. *The Red Book.* New York: W.W. Norton and Co., 2009.

_____, and Wolfgang Pauli. *The Interpretation of Nature and the Psyche.* New York: Bollingen Foundation, 1955.

Kalsched, Donald. *The Inner World of Trauma: Archetypal Defenses of the Personal Spirit.* London/New York: Routledge, 1996.

Kaufmann, W. trans. and ed. *Basic Writings of Nietzsche.* New York: Modern Library, 1968.

Kazantzakis, Nikos. *The Saviors of God: Spiritual Exercises.* New York: Simon and Schuster, 1960.

Kerényi, Karl. *Dionysos: Archetypal Image of Indestructible Life.* Translated by Ralph Manheim. Princeton, N.J.: Bollingen Series LXV 2, 1996.

Labouvie-Vief, G. "Affect Complexities and Views of the Transcendent." In *The Psychology of Mature Spirituality*, edited by Polly Young-Eisendrath and Melvin E. Miller. London: Routledge, 2000, 103-119.

Lammers, Ann. *In God's Shadow: The Collaboration of Victor White and C.G. Jung.* New York: Paulist Press, 1994.

Larkin, Philip. *Collected Poems.* London: Farrar, Straus, Giroux, 1988.

Lao Tzu. *Tao Te Ching*. Translated by D. C. Lau. Baltimore, Maryland: Penguin Books Inc., 1963.

Leichsenring, Falk, and Sven Rabung. "Effectiveness of LTPP: A Meta-analysis," *Journal of the American Medical Association*, 2008, 300(13), 1551-1565.

Levertov, Denise. "Matins." In *Poems 1960-1967*. New York: New Directions Publishing Corporation, 1966.

Lewis, Thomas, Fari Amini, and Richard Lannon. *A General Theory of Love*. New York: Random House, Inc., 2000.

Lewis-Williams, David and David Pearce. *Inside the Neolithic Mind: Consciousness, Cosmos and the Realm of the Gods*. London: Thames and Hudson Ltd., 2005.

Linehan, Marsha. *Cognitive-Behavioral Treatment of Borderline Personality Disorder*. New York: Guilford Press, 1993.

Loy Ching-Yuen. *The Book of the Heart: Embracing the Tao*. Boston: Shambhala Publications, 1988.

Magid, Barry. *Ending the Pursuit of Happiness*. Boston: Wisdom Publications, Inc., 2008.

Main, Roderick. "Numinosity and Terror: Jung's Psychological Revision of Otto as an Aid to Engaging Religious Fundamentalism." In *The Idea of the Numinous*, edited by Ann Casement and David Tacey. East Sussex, U.K.: Routledge, 2006, 159-160.

Mallon, Ted. *The Journey Toward Masterful Philanthropy*. Boulder, Colorado: Five Centuries Press, 2004.

Mansfield, Victor. *Synchronicity, Science and Soul Making*. Chicago: Open Court, 1995.

Marlan, Stanton. *The Black Sun*. College Station: Texas A & M University Press, 2005.

_____. ed. *Archetypal Psychologies: Reflections in Honor of James Hillman*. New Orleans: Spring Journal Books, 2008.

Maslow, Abraham. *The Highest State of Consciousness*. New York: Doubleday, 1972.

McGehee, Pittman. *The Three Threads of Individuation: Biological, Psychological, and Mythological*. Houston: The Jung Center of Houston Bookstore, audiotape, 2000.

McNeely, Deldon. *Touching*. Toronto: Inner City Books, 1987.

_____. *Animus Aeternus*. Toronto: Inner City Books, 1991.

_____. "Walking the Crooked Mile," *Philosophy & Psychology, Spring Journal 77*. New Orleans: Spring Journal, 2008.

Meier, C. A., ed. *Atom and Archetype: The Pauli/Jung Letters, 1932-1958.* Princeton, N.J.: Princeton University Press, 2001.

Meissner, W.W. "On Putting a Cloud in a Bottle: Psychoanalytic Perspectives on Mysticism," *Psychoanalytic Quarterly* LXXIV, 2005.

Merton, Thomas. *Conjectures of a Guilty Bystander,* quoted in Merton, *A Merton Reader,* 345, quoted in Cynthia Bourgeault, *Mystical Hope Trusting in the Mercy of God,* Cambridge, Massachusetts: Cowley Publications, 2001, 36.

Miller, Arthur. *Einstein, Picasso: Space, Time and the Beauty that Causes Havoc.* New York: Basic Books, 2001.

Miller, David. "Nothing Almost Sees Miracles! Self and No-Self in Psychology and Religion," *Journal of Psychology and Religion,* 4-5, 1995, 1-25.

Morgan, Vance. *Weaving the World: Simone Weil on Science, Mathematics, and Love.* University of Notre Dame Press, 2005.

Nagy, Marilyn. *Philosophical Issues in the Psychology of C.G. Jung.* New York: SUNY Press, 1991.

Needleman, Jacob. *A Little Book on Love.* New York: Dell Publishing, 1996.

Nicoll, Maurice. *The New Man.* Boulder: Shambhala Press, 1984.

Odajnyk, W. *Jung and Politics: The Political and Social Ideas of C.G. Jung.* New York: New York University Press, 1976.

Parsons, Michael. "Mankind's Attempt to Understand Itself: Psychoanalysis and Its Relation to Science and Religion." *fort da* (2005), 11, (2), 18-33.

Penrose, Roger. *The Large, the Small, the Human Mind.* Cambridge: Cambridge University Press, 1997.

Pearce, Joseph Chilton. *The Biology of Transcendence.* Rochester, Vermont: Park Street Press, 2002.

Piercy, Marge. *The Moon is Always Female.* New York: Alfred A. Knopf, 1985.

Progoff, Ira. *Depth Psychology and Modern Man.* New York: Julian Press, 1959.

Raff, Jeffrey. *Jung and the Alchemical Imagination.* York Beach, ME: Nicholas-Hayes, Inc., 2000.

Reagan, Michael, ed. *The Hand of God: Thoughts and Images Reflecting the Spirit of the Universe.* Radnor, Pennsylvania: Templeton Foundation Press, 1999.

Redfearn, Joseph. *My Self, My Many Selves.* London: Karnac Books, 1994.

Rilke, Rainer Maria. *Selected Poems of Rainer Maria Rilke.* Trans. by Robert Bly. New York: Harper and Row, 1981.

Rossi, Ernest. "Creativity and the Notion of the Numinosum." *Body and Soul, Spring Journal 72*, 2005.

Rowland, Susan. *Jung as a Writer.* New York: Routledge, 2005.

Samuels, Andrew. *Jung and the Post-Jungians.* London: Routledge and Keegan Paul, 1985.

_____. Bani Shorter, and Fred Plaut, eds. *A Critical Dictionary of Jungian Analysis.* London: Routledge and Keegan Paul, 1986.

_____. *The Plural Psyche: Personality, Morality and the Father.* London, Routledge, 1989.

_____. *The Political Psyche.* London: Routledge, 1993.

Scholem, Gershom. *Alchemy and Kabbalah.* Putnam, Connecticut: Spring, Inc., 2006.

Schore, Allan. "The Effect of Early Relational Trauma on Right Brain Development, Affect Regulation, and Infant Mental Health," *Infant Mental Health Journal,* 2001.

Scientific American Special Issue: "Better Brains." *Scientific American,* September, 2003.

Shamdasani, Sonu. *Jung and the Making of Modern Psychology: The Dream of a Science.* Cambridge: Cambridge University Press, 2003.

Sharp, Daryl. *Jung Lexicon: A Primer of Terms and Concepts.* Toronto: Inner City Books, 1990.

Slater, Glen. "Cyborgian Drift: Resistance is not Futile." *Psyche and Nature, Vol. 1, Spring Journal 75,* 2006.

Smith, C. Michael. *Jung and Shamanism in Dialogue.* Mahwah, N.J.: Paulist Press, 1997.

Smith, Curtis D. *Jung's Quest for Wholeness: A Religious and Historical Perspective.* New York: SUNY Press, 1990.

Smolin, Lee. *The Trouble with Physics.* Boston: Houghton Mifflin Company, 2006.

Spiegelman, J. Marvin, and Miyuki, Mokusen. *Buddhism and Jungian Psychology.* Tempe, AZ: New Falcons Publications, 1985.

Spiegelman, J. Marvin. *The Unhealed Healer: Reich, Jung, Regardie and Me.* Scottsdale, AZ: New Falcons Publications, 1992.

Stein, Murray. "Individuation: Inner Work," *Journal of Jungian Theory and Practice 7* no. 2, 2005.

_____. *The Principle of Individuation.* Wilmette, IL: Chiron Publications, 2006.

_____. "'Divinity expresses the Self...' An Investigation," *The Journal of Analytical Psychology*, 2008, 53, 305-327.

Steiner, Rudolf. *The Course of My Life*. New York: Anthroposophic Press, 1951.

Stephens, Barbara. "The Martin Buber-Carl Jung Disputations," *The Journal of Analytical Psychology*, 2001, 46, 3, 455-91.

_____. "The Return of the Prodigal: The Emergence of Jungian Themes in Post-Freudian Thought." *The Journal of Analytical Psychology*, 1999, 44, 197-220.

Stevens-Long, Judith. "The Prism Self: Multiplicity on the Path to Transcendence," in Young-Eisendrath, P., ed. *The Psychology of Mature Spirituality*, 2000.

Tacey, David. Lecture to The International Association for Jungian Studies, "The Psyche's Sacredness and the Rebirth of Imagination at the End of Modernity," Greenwich, England, 2007.

Tarnas, Richard. *Cosmos and Psyche*. New York: Penguin Books, 2006.

Taylor, Jill. *My Stroke of Insight*. New York: Viking, 2008.

Thich Nhat Hanh. *Peace is Every Step*. New York: Bantam Books, 1992.

Verene, Donald Phillip. "Coincidence, historical repetition, and self-knowledge: Jung, Vico, and Joyce." *The Journal of Analytical Psychology* 47, no. 3, 2002.

von Franz, Marie-Louise. *Interpretation of Fairy Tales*. Toronto: Inner City Books, 1970.

_____. *Number and Time*. Evanston: Northwestern University Press, 1974.

Waide, John. "The Making of Self and World in Advertising." *Journal of Business Ethics* 6. no. 2/February 87, 73-79.

Watkins, Mary. *Invisible Guests*. Hillsdale, NJ: The Analytic Press, 1986.

Watts, Alan. *Psychotherapy East and West*, New York: Random House, 1961.

_____. *The Way of Zen*. New York: Vintage Books, 1957.

Weil, Simone. *Gravity and Grace*. London, Routledge, 2002.

Wheelwright, Jane. *For Women Growing Older*. Houston: C.G. Jung Educational Center, 1984.

Whitmont, Christopher. *The Symbolic Quest: Basic Concepts of Analytical Psychology*. Princeton: Princeton University Press, 1978.

Wilbur, Ken. *Quantum Questions: Mystical Writings of the World's Greatest Physicists*. Boston: Shambhala, 2001.

Wood, James. "The Unforgotten," *The New Yorker*, July 28, 2008.

Young-Eisendrath, Polly and Terence Dawson. *The Cambridge Companion to Jung*. Cambridge: Cambridge University Press, 1997.

_____ and M. E. Miller, eds. *The Psychology of Mature Spirituality*. London: Routledge, 2000.

_____ and Shoji Muramoto, eds. *Awakening and Insight: Zen Buddhism and Psychotherapy*. Hove, East Sussex: Brunner-Routledge, 2002.

References to *The Collected Works of C.G. Jung*, translated by R.F.C. Hull, edited by H. Read, M. Fordham, G. Adler, and W. McGuire, published in America by Princeton University Press, Bollingen Series XX, 1953-1992, are denoted in the text by the name of the essay, then as CW, followed by the volume number and paragraph number. Other publications by Jung are listed by name and volume.

INDEX

Y

Z

Rahsaan Roland Kirk
Petite Fleur